ORYOKI AND THE ORYOKI CHANT

INCLUDING
THE SUTRA OF THE RECOLLECTION OF THE NOBLE THREE JEWELS
AND
THE TIBETAN MONASTIC MEAL LITURGY
AND FULL COMMENTARIES TO THEM

BY TONY DUFF
PADMA KARPO TRANSLATION COMMITTEE

Lydian and Palatino typefaces. Palatino typeface with diacritical marks designed and created by Tony Duff, Tibetan Computer Company.
http://www.tibet.dk/tcc

First edition, 5th November, 2008

ISBN 978-9937-9031-0-3

Produced, Printed, and Published by
Padma Karpo Translation Committee
PO Box 4957
Kathmandu
NEPAL

Committee Members for this book:
Tony Duff
Christopher Duff
Boyce Tech

Web-site and e-mail contact through:
http://www.tibet.dk/pktc
Or search Padma Karpo Translation Committee on the web.

Table of Contents

Introduction

Food and everything involved with it is a major part of human life, one that cannot be avoided. Because of this, Buddhists in general have looked for ways to bring meal times into practice and have developed various disciplines for doing so. The monastic traditions of Buddhism in particular have developed highly formalized ways of taking meals. These formal, monastic ways of taking food have a great advantage. They provide a chance to bring eating, which otherwise easily slips into a mindless affair, into practice. They accomplish this by providing a container that allows the mind of practice to be kept, and even to be developed further, during a meal.

The monastic tradition of Tibetan Buddhism has a formal way of eating and it was used in Tibetan Buddhist monasteries before the calamity in 1959. However, Tibetan Buddhism primarily followed the Vajra Vehicle so, generally speaking, there was less focus on the outer formalities of monasticism and more focus on the inner disciplines of the Vajra Vehicle[1]. The monastic tradition of

---

[1] There are three levels of path in Tibetan Buddhism. They are called the Lesser, Great, and Vajra Vehicles. In Sanskrit, they are the Hinayana, Mahayana, and Vajrayana respectively. For a reference point, the Theravada of South-East Asia is one of

Japanese Buddhism, on the other hand, placed great emphasis on outer forms and, with that, developed a very formal way of eating meals that was regularly observed.

In the 1970's, the Vidyadhara Chogyam Trungpa Rinpoche was successfully transplanting Tibetan Buddhism into the West. He was teaching his disciples the original approach of his lineage, the Kagyu tradition, in which practitioners are lay people who follow the Vajra Vehicle. A person who practises this way is called a tantrika[2].

By 1980, his disciples had become well known for their embodiment of the view that goes with the tantrika approach. However, he was noticing that their discipline needed more attention. For example, he pointed out to them that they were losing their practice at meal times, even during intensive practice periods. At this point, his teaching took a new direction and he began to give more emphasis to the basic Buddhist disciplines of the Lesser Vehicle. He still did not want his disciples to be monks or nuns but did want them to be more connected with the basic disciplines of Buddhism that monks and nuns immerse themselves in. Therefore, in 1980, he instituted a monastic style of eating as the way for his disciples to take meals while they were doing intensive practice and in 1981 instituted the lay vows of a Buddhist as something to be taken by his disciples.

The Vidyadhara introduced the monastic style of eating with an innovation. There is a Japanese style of monastic

---

the schools of the Lesser Vehicle.

[2] The Tibetan equivalent is "ngag pa".

eating called "Oryoki". He took the form of Japanese Oryoki, joined the Tibetan monastic meal liturgy to it, and taught it with the view of his lineage of Tibetan Buddhism—the view of the three vehicles.

I had been a monk in the Tibetan tradition and lived in a monastery for several years during the 1970's. When the Vidyadhara introduced the monastic style of eating, I found it to be personally very suitable and immediately took great interest in it. It seemed natural to learn the whole system and I soon found myself in the role of head server during a string of dathuns done at Rocky Mountain Dharma Centre, as it was then called, during late 1980 and early 1981. After that, I was happy to obtain a position as head server at the 1982 seminary, then Oryoki Master at the 1983 seminary, and Oryoki advisor in subsequent seminaries.

During the early 1980's, the Vidyadhara gave many teachings on the new practice of Oryoki and a great deal of advice on how it should be taken as practice within the community. Because of my extensive involvement with dathuns, seminary, and practice in Boulder at the time, I heard these teachings personally or received them through people such as Ani Pema Chodron, who was also in close communication with the Vidyadhara and intimately involved with practice matters then. My very active role in the Nalanda Translation Committee during those years contributed further to my knowledge of Oryoki and how the Vidyadhara saw it within the community. Later, in 1985 and 1986, I was asked to oversee Oryoki at the seminaries of those years, and to ensure that all the knowledge that I had accumulated was passed on to the servers and head servers of the time.

An oral tradition developed during those years that kept and transmitted all the details of the practice. However, one thing that was missing was an explanation of the liturgy used for the practice. While listening to the Vidyadhara teach the first part of the liturgy—a section called *The Sutra of the Recollection of the Noble Three Jewels*—at the 1982 Vajradhatu Seminary, and hearing his many comments on how Oryoki should be taken as practice, it came to mind that I should write a full explanation of the liturgy and how to use it. A draft was started during my position as Oryoki Master to Seminary in 1983 and work on it continued during my roles as advisor to Oryoki in the 1985 and 1986 Seminaries. The draft was never brought to final publication, though it did leak out in the late 1980's.

The leakage came to my attention this year, as I was preparing to translate Ju Mipham's commentary on the sutra mentioned above. Ju Mipham's commentary was the same one that the Vidyadhara relied on for his own understanding and teaching of the sutra when he was a young man in Tibet and later, when he taught it at Seminary in 1982. The coincidence of the situation prompted me to complete the work and this is the outcome.

As I took up the task of completing the work, I reflected on my experience that the mention of "Oryoki" usually conjures up the physical form of the practice. However, Oryoki is much more than that. It is a practice that involves the whole person. It has a physical form for the body, a liturgy for the speech, and a view for the mind involved with the practice. In regard to that, this book is not a how-to-do-it manual of the physical form of Oryoki. In the opinion of a number of us who have been closely involved with the practice, the details of the outer form are best transmitted orally. We feel that there are good reasons for not committing them to writing. Let me say here that I hope they are not. However, the liturgy does need to be studied in order to be understood and likewise, so does the view. Therefore, this book is primarily about the monastic meal liturgy that the Vidyadhara selected for use with Oryoki practice and, to go with that, has plenty of discussion of the view and how it is put together with the practice.

The Vidyadhara had called his community "Vajradhatu". After his passing, the community was taken over by his son, called the "Sakyong", and he has renamed the community "Shambhala". The book began as a presentation of Oryoki that followed the Vidyadhara's way of teaching it for his Vajradhatu community. However, at this later time of completing the work, the Buddha's teaching has spread widely across the globe and there is interest in Oryoki amongst Westerners from communities other than the Japanese Zen and Shambhala communities. Therefore, the book additionally addresses the possibility that it could be practised by other communities, too.

As I began to write more inclusively, I came to realize that this was no doubt part of the Vidyadhara's original intent. He worked to propagate teachings that would promote basic sanity across the earth, and in forms that would benefit a wide audience, not just those practising the very defined path of a particular tradition of Tibetan Buddhism. Hopefully, I have included enough in the book so that anyone interested could take a step towards turning meals into practice using what is here. However, if you would like to make "Oryoki" into something that you or your community could use for practice, please do not hesitate to contact me for further assistance.

During my close involvement with Oryoki in the 1980's, I consulted many people to learn more about the practice and liturgy. The explanations here are based on instructions received directly and indirectly from the Vidyadhara, Chogyam Trungpa Rinpoche, and help provided by the Venerable Traleg Khyabgon Rinpoche, the Venerable Thrangu Rinpoche, and Zasep Tulku Rinpoche. My close relations with Ani Pema Chodron and Mr. Larry Mermelstein of the Nalanda Translation Committee also added to my knowledge. Then, and very importantly, there were the people from whom I learned Oryoki, both the personal and serving practices; they included Sally Symanski and the various Oryoki Masters of seminary who instructed me before graduating to that position myself—Robert Salskov, Roland Cohen, and Giannina Jobson in that order. I thank all of my teachers with an expression of only the greatest appreciation for what they passed on and their time spent teaching it. Thanks to all of them!

Lama Tony Duff
6th November 2008,
Swayambhu,
Nepal

The Development of Oryoki

The various forms, liturgical procedures, and views surrounding the eating of food in all Buddhist traditions were developed from the teachings and methodologies given to the sangha in India by Lord Buddha, two and a half thousand years ago. The physical form of eating started with the begging bowl, which was established by the Buddha as one of the three requisites which a monk or nun received at ordination. The bowl had to be cared for in a particular way and was not allowed to be given away to others. In this are seen the roots of the sacredness of an Oryoki set, and the implication that owning such a set is a sign of someone who has taken refuge and entered the life of a Buddhist practitioner.

Over a period of centuries, the sangha settled down from being a loosely-knit group of wandering ascetics and formed large monastic centres. In some places the simple begging bowl developed into a small eating set consisting of a bowl, a cloth, and an eating utensil. At the same time, the simple instructions on such matters as eating were codified and developed into liturgies, and a whole practice of monastic eating was developed. This was the state of affairs in China when Dogen Zenji arrived from Japan many centuries ago.

Dogen Zenji had studied Buddhism with several teachers in Japan but felt that he wasn't getting the essence, so he undertook the rather dangerous sea journey to China where Chan Buddhism was flourishing. After many difficulties, he found a teacher with whom he studied and practised, and who gave him the complete transmission of Chan. He also learned the ways of a Buddhist monk, including the monastic eating practice being used in China at the time. He returned to Japan where he instituted that style of eating. At some point, the Zen masters of the Soto Zen tradition refined the practice into one with highly detailed form. That form was called "Oryoki".

The monastic eating practices of the Japanese and Tibetan traditions of Buddhism have the same source and both have a similar view, thus, taken overall, there are not many differences in how they conduct their monastic meals. However, the form of Oryoki is much more detailed than the form used in Tibetan monastic tradition. For example, Oryoki requires a whole set of bowls, wrapped in several cloths whereas Tibetans have a simple bowl of their own choice wrapped in whatever cloth is to hand and a spoon to eat with. Furthermore, Oryoki has very strict forms for dispensing and eating the food where the Tibetan form is much looser.

Both traditions use a liturgy derived from the teachings of the Buddha to go with these meals. Tibetan monasteries use a liturgy that begins with a sutra called *The Sutra of the Recollection of the Noble Three Jewels* which is a development of a Lesser Vehicle teaching given by the Buddha in the first turning of the Wheel of Dharma and common to all Buddhists, a teaching called "The Six Recollections".

In the 1970's, the form of Oryoki as practised in the Soto Zen lineage was transmitted to the Vidyadhara Chogyam Trungpa Rinpoche by Kobenchino Roshi. The Vidyadhara felt that the detailed form of Oryoki made it an excellent vehicle for his students to train themselves in shamatha and vipashyana while eating. However, a liturgy from the Tibetan system was needed for it, thus, in 1980, the Vidyadhara had his Nalanda Translation Committee translate one into English. It is the liturgy that is presented and explained in this book. The Vidyadhara then amalgamated the Japanese form of Oryoki with the Tibetan liturgy and introduced this new form of ancient practice to his community for the first time at the 1980 Vajradhatu seminary. There, he commanded that, henceforth, all practice gatherings of his community should use this practice of monastic eating as the way of taking meals. Thus was born the Oryoki tradition of the Vajradhatu, now Shambhala, sangha. In it, the strong outer form of Japanese Oryoki is practised with the Tibetan liturgy and all of that within the views of the three vehicles.

In this new style of Oryoki practice, the Oryoki set and the procedures for using it come directly from the Japanese tradition. There is a leader of the meal and, if the gathering is large, a chant-master. The phases of the meal are signalled by the leader using a "gaṇḍi" which is a long billet of hardwood of certain size and design which is struck in a certain way with a hardwood striker. The gaṇḍi is a device prescribed in the Vinaya for calling the monastic sangha to events and for indicating the beginning and so forth of those events. Its design, use, and the rhythms in which it is struck go back to the earliest days of monastic Buddhism.

The seating arrangements in the new style vary, though there has been an attempt to have the rows arranged perpendicularly to the shrine in accordance with general Buddhist monastic tradition. In the new style, there is the cook's offering of Japanese Oryoki; this has a Tibetan equivalent but is done in the Japanese manner. In the new style, there is some drumming involved which is done in Tibetan monastic style. In the new style, a few other developments have occurred to accommodate the practice environment, such as the design and production of small "Oryoki tables", which were designed within Vajradhatu but inspired by Japanese monastic tradition. These Oryoki tables are wooden, about three inches high, and slightly wider than tall, being about twenty inches long. They are large enough to accommodate the Oryoki set nicely when it has been fully opened and set out. They are painted with black enamel.

In the 1980's, the Oryoki tradition was officially preserved by today's Sakyong who had the position of "Sawang" at the time. Several people, notably the seminary Oryoki Masters, made efforts to keep the lineages of the form and liturgical procedures alive and developing without becoming polluted. Those people, in order of appearance from 1980 through to 1987—Robert Salskov, Roland Cohen, Giannina Jobson, Tony Duff, John Sennhauser, and Ane Tsultrim Chotso—along with Ani Pema Chodron who was the seminary Practice Coordinator for several years, are good reference points for information about Oryoki as it was taught and developed under the eye of the Vidyadhara.

A word of warning perhaps should be sounded here. It has been and is still a point of concern amongst those who have been intimately involved with transmission of the lineage of practice of Oryoki that corruption can easily seep in. I remember the story of the head cook of the 1985 seminary. He was a professional cook, trained in the high kitchens of chef-dom. In prior years, the head cook had always been a senior student, one who had been to seminary and was already a well-trained person within the Vidyadhara's community. However, that year, it had been hard to find a head cook and the administration had accepted the chef, despite his lack of practice, as the head cook. His lack of practice coupled with his very strong-minded attitudes coming from the kitchens he had trained in soon had him at odds with the head server of that year. Unfortunately, he used his position to bully his opinions about and several times insisted on pushing new ideas about the form of Oryoki into place. He insisted that Oryoki was all about eating elegantly—in a very worldly sense—which it is not and never has been. As I heard of these things, I encouraged the head server not to give ground but there were tremors, nonetheless. Similarly, I remember going to one practice location within Vajradhatu in the late 1980's and being told not to turn my back to the shrine when serving. The atmosphere in that place was very theistic and quite the reverse of the atmosphere that the Vidyadhara had engendered while he was alive. Corruption of the view creeps in slowly—it comes as a little change here and a little change there by people who do not have the full view and who find a way to insert their particular neuroses. Because of this, some have felt that a full manual of Oryoki, with all the details of the form should be produced. However, many of us who have been in the position of transmitting the lineage of Oryoki have felt otherwise, despite knowing that the details of the tradition do get corrupted. Somehow, the oral tradition is very important and should be the reference point.

The basic view of Oryoki that the Vidyadhara laid out to his students was like this. For him, Oryoki was an important way to put Lesser Vehicle discipline firmly into his community. His community was one of tantrikas not monastics but he saw that the basic discipline that monastics carry was needed for his students and he stated very clearly that Oryoki was an important way of bringing that into the community. At the same time, and as he brought to the attention of everyone at the 1982 seminary, Oryoki in the Japanese Zen tradition is not only a monastic, disciplined way of eating food but also has the possibility of being a very advanced practice and does have an inner teaching associated with it. That inner practice is not given to beginners; it is only given to those who are deeply involved with the path. Similarly, he pointed out, anyone who has progressed to Vajra Vehicle practice could and should practise Oryoki with the secret view of the Vajra Vehicle. And of them, those who are far enough advanced in the view of Vajra Vehicle would understand that Oryoki can be a way of joining all three vehicles, none missing or downplayed, into one coherent practice.

In other words, Oryoki the way that the Vidyadhara taught it is done with the view of the three vehicle approach of Tibetan Buddhism. Thus, when Oryoki is practised in the Shambhala community, the three vehicle approach, or its equivalent called the nine vehicle approach[3], is the way that view is to be applied to the practice. Nonetheless, the possibility that it can be taken as three vehicle practice should not turn into a deprecation, or loss even, of the monastic aspect. The Vidyadhara emphasized that his community should not lose the monastic feel of the practice and its connection to renunciation, taking refuge, and the other basic disciplines of Buddhism. The Vidyadhara made it very clear that the practice of Oryoki was a form of monastic practice for his community, a practice intimately connected with the basic matters of discipline and personal emancipation.

The Vidyadhara's emphasis on Oryoki's importance not just as a meal practice but as an integral part of a whole Lesser Vehicle discipline that he was trying to create for his community is highlighted by what he expressed to Ani Pema Chodron at the Vajradhatu 1983 seminary. He said that, in the Vajradhatu sangha, a student should not be allowed to own an Oryoki set until he or she had for-

---

[3] The nine vehicles is how the first teachings of Buddhism to come into Tibet, now upheld by the Nyingma tradition, are encapsulated. The three vehicles is how the teachings of the second wave of Buddhism that came into Tibet, now upheld by the Sakya, Kagyu, and Gelug traditions, are encapsulated. The nine vehicles have Dzogchen as their highest view, the three vehicles have Mahāmudrā as their highest view but from a broad perspective, the two are essentially the same presentation.

mally taken refuge. He said that the refuge ceremony should come to include the formal presentation of an Oryoki set to the new refugee by the preceptor. This is particularly interesting as this style would echo the manner in which a monk receives his bowl from the preceptor during ordination, and it certainly carries with it the sense that one's Oryoki set is an integral part of one's practice life and moreover is a particularly sacred belonging.

This command was a brilliant idea and is worthy of attention. At the time of ordination, a monk undertakes a set of vows. He is given the few possessions specifically allowed for a monk. In particular, he is given his robes and begging bowl. From that time on, the robes and begging bowl are very meaningful signs for himself and others of what he has entered and undertaken. Similarly, according to the Vidyadhara, the lay Tibetan Buddhist in Vajradhatu was to take refuge and receive his Oryoki set at the time. The Oryoki set would then not be just another thing that a person has to have to do Oryoki—which is often the status it is given. Rather, it would be a very personal item that signified to all that the person had taken refuge and formally entered the community of Buddhists. It would also be a reminder of the set of vows that he had taken at the time of refuge and of the discipline he had entered because of it. Oryoki, the way that the Vidyadhara wanted it to be, really was part of living the disciplines of the Lesser Vehicle as a layman, not only a way to eat meals as practice.

The Liturgy for Oryoki

Source of the Liturgy

The Tibetan monastic meal liturgy is a very old one whose origin is not well known. These days, there are several versions of the liturgy. The one chosen by the Vidyadhara Chogyam Trungpa for the practice of Oryoki comes from a standard compilation of liturgies put together by Dudjom Jigdrel Yeshe Dorje Rinpoche[4]. It is the source for the original translation done by Nalanda Translation Committee and the new translation contained in this book.

Differences can be seen amongst the various editions of the liturgy. There are minor variations in the wording of the sutra that begins the liturgy because of differences in the ways that the early Tibetan translators chose to translate specific terms. Also, different selections of dedica-

[4] Dudjom Rinpoche was a very great Nyingma master of Tibetan Buddhism who lived in the twentieth century and who was well-known for his realization and knowledge.

tion prayers are used at the end of the liturgy. However, the basic liturgy remains the same in each case.

Style of the Liturgy

The liturgy is for monastic eating so it presents Lesser Vehicle teaching and emphasizes Lesser Vehicle ways. The Great Vehicle approach is not really written into the liturgy; there is a small mention of bodhisatvas[5] in the dedications at the end but there is no mention of anything that is strictly Great Vehicle and that would not fit with someone who followed only the Lesser Vehicle. Similarly, the Vajra Vehicle approach is not really written into the liturgy though there is an inclusion of offerings to the three roots—the gurus, yidams, and dharmapalas—that does come from the Vajra Vehicle approach of Tibetan Buddhism. If there were one thing in the liturgy that might have to be changed for use in non-Tibetan Buddhist communities, it would be just this. The change would be very minor though.

Thus, this liturgy embodies the Lesser Vehicle, the lowest common denominator for all Buddhists. At the moment, it is used primarily in the West within the Shambhala community with their Oryoki practice but it could be used by anyone following the Tibetan Buddhist way, regardless of their level of practice. Moreover, it could be used in any Buddhist community not only in Tibetan

---

[5] This is the spelling that is considered to be correct in the Tibetan tradition, that was established by the great Tibetan translators and their Indian scholar-advisors at the time of Padmasambhava.

ones, possibly with some minor modification to the offering sections as just mentioned.

View and Practice with the Liturgy

This section points out that the liturgy is from the Lesser Vehicle but that any level of Buddhist view could be put with it. The various views are not taught as part of Oryoki practice *per se* but are learned by the practitioner and brought to the practice of Oryoki with the aid of the liturgy. Anyone teaching Oryoki will show the students how to join the outer form and the meaning of the liturgy with the level of view that the students either have or are training in at the time.

The highest view of Tibetan Buddhism is the view of the Vajra Vehicle and Tibetan Buddhism has the special feature of emphasizing that all three vehicles can be successfully practised together. The Vidyadhara Chogyam Trungpa taught this approach in general and did teach it as the way for his students to practise Oryoki. His comments about Oryoki at the end of the last chapter come from this special feature of Tibetan Buddhism that all three vehicles can be practised together. They present the possibility that a Lesser Vehicle practice could be done while maintaining its Lesser Vehicle style but bringing it under the umbrella of all three vehicles. The traditional Tibetan way of explaining how that would be done with Oryoki would go something like this: the discipline of the outer form would be Lesser Vehicle; the inner intention would be the bodhichitta of the Great Vehicle; and the view held during the practise of Oryoki would be that of the Vajra Vehicle.

The ultimate way of doing Oryoki is to join the forms and practices with reality seen in direct perception. What that means will differ according to which school of Buddhism the practitioner is following and which level of practice he is doing within that. The Vidyadhara Chogyam Trungpa taught his students that the ultimate way of joining three vehicle practice to Oryoki is to experience the whole three vehicle journey on the spot as Oryoki is done. This is something that practitioners who have been properly entered into the Vajra Vehicle will understand and be able to apply to Oryoki. Those who are following the three vehicle journey of Tibetan Buddhism but who have not entered the Vajra Vehicle yet will be able to do Oryoki with the view of Great Vehicle or Lesser Vehicle, according to their level of training. Practitioners in other communities can, similarly, bring their own view to the practice. For example, followers of the Theravada could easily take the liturgy and work with it literally because its literal expression embodies their view, which is that of the Lesser Vehicle.

In fact, the categorization of dharma into Lesser, Great, and Vajra vehicles—or any other category or division that you could think of—is artificial. These categories and divisions come from reality being cut up, intellectually, into chunks for the sole purpose of helping practitioners to arrive at the direct perception of reality that is the true dharma. In fact, there is only one true dharma, the dharma of reality itself and this dharma then appears as the many conventions taught as "Buddhist dharma". When you can cut to the state of reality that the conventional dharmas point at, you arrive at the final view that transcends all views of "Lesser Vehicle", "Great Vehicle",

"Vajra Vehicle", and so on. As Trungpa Rinpoche taught it—and in fact as any teacher of the Tibetan tradition would have to teach it—that is the meaning of the three vehicle journey being experienced on the spot. And, in any tradition at all of Buddhism, that is the meaning of the view of that tradition being experienced on the spot. It is possible to practise Oryoki like this. Doing so takes it beyond a practice that belongs to a specific tradition and specific view. That universal possibility was firmly presented by the Vidyadhara even though he used the three vehicle way of talking about it. In fact, it is the goal of Oryoki that the outer form and the use of the liturgy should become expressions of mind that is seeing the true view directly.

Oryoki as it is usually presented starts with enormous attention to the outer form. After that, and a step inward, there should be a clear explanation of the liturgy and the ways in which it engages the speech and rational mind. This step has not happened well in Shambhala venues to date because the liturgy has not been well understood; the purpose of this book is to rectify that. Finally, there is a discussion of how the form should be done in conjunction with the view. This approach is the outside going in approach, which is referred to in the highest teachings of Tibetan Buddhism as the bottom going up approach. It is very much the style of sutra practice and especially of Lesser Vehicle practice. You are in samsara and are trying to get out, so you deal with your grossest aspect first, your body, followed by the next grossest one, your speech, and only then do you consider mind. This approach to Oryoki practice makes it yet another of the many skilful means available in Buddhism whose real meaning is to get you to be in the view, directly perceived, of reality. When that happens, that realization of the view on the spot becomes the ruling principle that guides, informs, and actually produces the outer form and the concepts of the liturgy. That is the inside going out or top going down, as it is called, approach. The top going down approach is the hallmark of the Vajra Vehicle.

The liturgy itself is categorized as "Lesser Vehicle" dharma nevertheless it does point at the reality that the Buddha himself realized, which itself is the ultimate dharma that transcends all the divisions that we have just been talking about. The sutra at the beginning of the liturgy makes this point over and again. For example, it says, "The dharma taught by the bhagavat is properly revealed in the Vinaya". Some people might find themselves thinking that this is a Lesser Vehicle teaching with a great emphasis on monastic approach and that the constant teaching that appears in connection with this in the Vinaya, the code of monastic life, is good dharma but not the actual dharma. They might think that Oryoki somehow is useful but is not really getting to the essence of the teaching because of the monastic emphasis. This way of thinking is one that happens very easily to practitioners who have been exposed to the Vajra Vehicle and to people who do not have an affinity for monastic ways. All in all, they are thinking, "Oh, this is about renunciation; it is not really about the highest view". However, a full explanation of the sutra shows that even renunciation itself, as the epitome of the monastic approach, is actually a perfect expression of the ultimate view. More is said about this in the complete explanation of the sutra, later in the book.

Again, the sutra at the beginning of the liturgy points out that the dharma teaching is "without disharmony". The apparently lower teachings of monastic practice contained in the liturgy are fully consistent with the highest teachings of Buddhism, even though they might seem to be contradictory on the surface. Immediately after that, the sutra points out that not only are all teachings of dharma consistent but that dharma in general "has inclusion" meaning that each individual teaching includes the meaning of all dharma. Thus, the various monastic features of the liturgy are not only consistent with higher teachings even if they seem contradictory to them but more than that, each one also contains in it the entirety of the Buddha's teaching. Thus, at the time of practice, the liturgy does have the capacity to bring the views of all vehicles, categories, and divisions of dharma, regardless of what they are, together on the spot.

As an aside, the last paragraphs illustrate the depth of meaning available through the use of the liturgy and Oryoki practice. The sutra, which is read at the start of each Oryoki session, is generally considered to be a way of arousing faith and taking refuge in the Three Jewels but it is also a great lesson in the Buddha's dharma and parts of it in particular help to set the view for the practice, as just shown. Whenever you do Oryoki using this liturgy, you not only get to include meals in your practice in a general way but get to have an extensive and possibly very profound lesson on Buddhism every time!

All in all, the liturgy transcends all "vehicles" despite being a "Lesser Vehicle" teaching. It is in fact a teaching on reality that anyone and everyone can use and appreciate, regardless of their personal level of practice and regardless of which stream of Buddhism they follow.

Use of the Liturgy in other Buddhist Communities

The explanation of any given level of practice as a three vehicle journey and of the Vajra Vehicle approach that comes with it is a central theme of Vidyadhara Chogyam Trungpa's lineage of Tibetan Buddhism and is emphasized in this book. However, and as the Vidyadhara made clear, this should not overshadow the fact that Oryoki done as a form and the liturgy for recitation with it are Lesser Vehicle practices. Because of it, Oryoki as a form and the liturgy as a support can be used by anyone and in any Buddhist community. In other words, the three vehicle approach of Tibetan Buddhism is not the only way to do Oryoki practice; all levels of view and practice as found in the many different Buddhist communities can be mixed with it.

The paragraphs in the last section about how the apparently lower teachings of renunciation and monastic practice do embody the highest view are also reasons why the liturgy can work for all Buddhists. The liturgy transcends all "levels" of dharma practice and is in fact a teaching on reality that anyone and everyone can use and appreciate.

The outer forms of Oryoki are directed at the practice of shamatha-vipashyana, a practice which is common to all Buddhist practitioners, and the liturgy emphasizes Lesser Vehicle practice, a view which is common to all Buddhist communities and which does, as explained by the sutra in the liturgy, include the full understanding of the reality which the cause of the expression of dharma. Thus Oryoki can be used very successfully in any Buddhist community. I was recently approached by two separate Theravadin practice groups who became very interested in Oryoki as something they might adapt for the use of their own communities. They were particularly pleased at how the outer form fitted with their own style of shamatha-vipashyana practice and ways of discipline, and were delighted with the liturgy, which consists largely of a sutra that has many things in common with Theravada practice. They asked me to help them adapt the Oryoki practice designed by the Vidyadhara Chogyam Trungpa for his Tibetan Buddhist community to their own needs. I am sure that it can be done very successfully.

Oryoki and Feast Practice

The meal liturgy was designed for monastic use but this particular edition of it has a short piece from the Vajra Vehicle added after the monastic meal liturgy. It was selected and put there by Dudjom Rinpoche for the benefit of tantrikas who might want a simple way to add feast practice to the basic monastic eating practice set out in the liturgy. He took it from the Nyingma treasure whose name is mentioned in the colophon of the piece. To be clear, this addition is not used for monastic meals and hence not for general Oryoki practice. For that reason, it was not included in the original translation of the liturgy by Nalanda Translation Committee that has been in use within the Shambhala community till now. However, this book tries to include greater possibilities of Oryoki, as mentioned in the introduction, so it does provide a complete translation of the liturgy found in Dudjom Rinpoche's compilation, with his added piece in place at the end.

Anyone who has been properly entered into the Vajra Vehicle will have some understanding of how to apply the view of Vajra Vehicle to Oryoki. This is something that each person does for himself and has no effect on the rituals of the outer form or liturgy. In addition to application of the view, there are several specific Vajra Vehicle practices that can be done in relation to eating, whether in the context of formal Oryoki or not. One of them is to turn the eating into inner ganachakra, or feast, as part of the practice of a deity. There are many liturgies that could be added explicitly to the Oryoki for that purpose including the one appended by Dudjom Rinpoche. Those who have had the necessary empowerments and instructions could use it to help with turning Oryoki into the feast practice of a deity, in particular. It can be done by anyone who has empowerment into a deity mandala at the Anuttarayoga or Mahayoga levels but not otherwise. The piece starts immediately after the liturgy used for Oryoki and monastic meals with the words, "*Also, those who, having the yoga of a deity, would like to make eating into the revelry of the inner gaṇachakra…* ", and goes down to the very end of the whole liturgy.

Translation of the Liturgy

When I first started work on this book, it was my intention simply to use the translation already made by the

Nalanda Translation Committee and which has been used with Oryoki in the Shambhala community since 1980. Unfortunately, the many mistakes in the existing translation prevented the production of a correct commentary that matched the liturgy. Also, reading the sutra is supposed to lead mind in a certain direction but the original translation of it leads in the wrong direction in a number of places. Therefore, I have provided a new, more accurate translation of the entire sutra, used the existing translations of the verses following that with a few minor changes, then added the addendum mentioned earlier that was not in the original translation.

Some people will be irked by this because they will want the commentary on the sutra to match what they have been reciting for all these years. All I can do is say that I am sorry! I had that thought too; for the sake of all the practitioners who have said this liturgy so many times, it would have been very nice just to reproduce it and that was my wish. And of course, as a matter of respect for the Nalanda Translation Committee, of which I am also a member, it would have been nice just to use their translation. However, time has marched on, knowledge of Tibetan Buddhism increased, and changes are sometimes necessary.

On the other hand, this little feast of knowledge about the sutra and the rest of the liturgy should be of great interest to the many people who have wanted to know more about what they having been chanting for all these years. It is my respectful hope that the much improved translation of the sutra will cause the aging translation to be replaced by the one in this book. For those in other communities, I recommend that you use the liturgy presented in this book.

How to Chant the Liturgy

The liturgy was arranged so that chanting and understanding it will increase understanding of and faith in the Three Jewels. This should encourage you to use chanting of the liturgy as a way of progressing along the path.

Orgyan Lingpa, one of the main treasure revealers of Padmasambhava's treasures, advised that, "Reading … with the three facets of clear, correct, and pleasant pronunciation", is the best way to read a liturgy.

To have clear and correct pronunciation, you must have a mind that is not distracted and which is paying attention to the words at very least. By doing that much, you will be creating a habit of synchronizing body, speech, and mind, an essential practice right from the beginning of the Buddhist path. To be un-distracted, you must have mindfulness and alertness, the two key factors involved in development of shamatha. Thus, the chanting of the liturgy benefits from whatever shamatha practice you have done already and at the same time can be shamatha practice. To pay attention to the words and pronounce them properly, you need certain qualities of mind that are connected with vipashyana. So, similarly, your vipashyana practice from before assists with your pronunciation now and the very pronouncing of the words clearly and correctly now can assist the development of your vipashyana practice.

In addition to using clear and correct pronunciation as a way to further your shamatha-vipashyana practice, if you additionally practise at paying attention to the meaning of the words as you read, that will lead to the development of faith, prajñā, and the various aspects of mind involved with intelligence and precision, all of which are valuable good qualities to possess in general. Of them, faith is one of the five main doorways to all good qualities so the faith developed on the spot by this technique can lead to many other types of opening on the spot, too.

To have a pleasant pronunciation could be something that you do for yourself. It requires paying attention to the quality of your voice, which is yet another training in shamatha-vipashyana. However, it could also be something that you do for everyone else in the room. A good chant-master will set a tone and pace that becomes a line that everyone else in the room can hang their voices around. However, it is not only up to the chant-master to provide the right lead, it is also up to all the practitioners to mix their voices with the others so that there is a real chant occurring. When this is done, it is very pleasant to hear but more than that, can have a profound effect on the group. In order to join your voice with the others, you have to become part of the group and when you do that, your mind also becomes part of the group mind. That means that, if you have particularly good understanding of what you are doing or some opening of faith, etcetera, occurs, it can be passed on to others. Similarly, if you are having a really difficult day or you are someone with not much understanding, the good energy and understanding of others can come to you. The possibilities of this tuning in are really quite extraordinary and it is possible to gain major insights just by joining in with the chanting.

Thus, rather than chant the liturgy with poor attention to what is being said, try to be present and involved with the liturgy and its meaning as much as possible. Then all of the benefits mentioned above can come not only for yourself but for others, too. All in all, chanting is a way of training body, speech, and mind in a positive way.

A major portion of the liturgy involves chanting the *Sutra of the Recollection of the Noble Three Jewels*. The sutra explains the characteristics of each of the Three Jewels so you can gain a great deal of knowledge just by paying attention to those characteristics.

That knowledge can lead, as mentioned above, to faith. The Buddha mentioned three types of faith. When you pay attention to the meaning of the sutra as you chant it, you can get a faith that comes with a very clear understanding of the good qualities of the Jewels; it is called "lucid faith". You can get a faith that, because of seeing these good qualities clearly, has great trust in the Jewels; that is "trusting faith". And you can get a faith that, because of seeing and trusting like this, openly aspires to develop those good qualities for yourself; that is "aspiring faith". These faiths can lead to many openings. Most important though is trusting faith leading to the mind that takes refuge in the Three Jewels because taking refuge is the very root of the whole path, the one doorway through which all levels of the path can be reached. There is an enormous value to reciting the liturgy so that it does cause a mind of refuge to come forth.

All in all, you are strongly encouraged to be mindful of what you are saying each time, as opposed to just memorizing the text of the liturgy and repeating it by rote.

Composition of the Liturgy

The liturgy has five main parts:

1. First is a general preparation, which is a recollection of the qualities of the noble Three Jewels followed by taking refuge in them.
2. Next is accepting the food.
3. Next is blessing and offering the food, which includes the practice of eating.
4. Next, as one cleans up after the meal, the kindness of the donors of the meal is returned.
5. Finally, the merit is dedicated.

This layout follows a particular oral instruction, called "The Three Excellences[6]", on how to do any session of practice. The instruction says that, to bring any activity fully to the path, three excellences must be present: taking refuge and, for Great Vehicle practice, arousing bodhichitta) which is the preparation; the main part of actual practice; and dedication, which is the conclusion.

The first two parts of the liturgy are the preparation; they involve chanting selections that concern the practice of recollecting the good qualities of the Three Jewels, arousing faith in them, and taking refuge in them. If you are a Great Vehicle practitioner, you would also arouse bodhicitta either at this point or before the practice.

---

[6] Tib. dam pa gsum.

Parts three and four are the main part of the practice. Here, one should keep the view of reality to whatever extent it has been understood and can be practised. Part three of the liturgy begins by developing that view with a purification of perception into sacred outlook. That purified perception is maintained in part four together with all the details of eating. Although the whole practice requires shamatha-vipashyana, you could say that this is the section where the practice is shamatha-vipashyana.

The fourth and fifth parts are the conclusion in which you dedicate the merit from the practice.

Each person will practise according to his own understanding. However, for a Lesser Vehicle practitioner the three parts could be: taking refuge; doing the practice with an awareness of the impermanence, unsatisfactoriness, composite nature, and so on of things; and dedicating according to the literal meaning of the dedication prayers. For a Great Vehicle practitioner the three parts could be: taking refuge and arousing bodhichitta; doing the practice with either fictional and superfactual[7] bodhichittas to the extent he could manage; and dedicating according to the literal meaning of the dedication prayers but with the thought of dedicating the merit accumulated for the sake of truly complete enlightenment. For a Vajra Vehicle practitioner the three parts could be the same as for the Great Vehicle practitioner except that the practice throughout could be done with the view of the Vajra Vehicle.

---

[7] Newer, more accurate wordings for what used to be called "relative and absolute..."

Oryoki in Other Ways—and even Without Oryoki

Oryoki is usually explained beginning with the form and going inwards to mind, which is the approach of a person who is in samsara and wanting to get out. It is a very methodical approach that is exactly the style of the Lesser Vehicle. It is, on the surface, what Oryoki is about. A higher approach is to start from a more enlightened state of mind, then go out to concepts with the liturgy, then go on to the physical matter of the Oryoki form. This approach, in which there is trust that the mind is a repository of the good qualities of enlightenment and that these good qualities are available, at least to some extent, on the spot, is the thrust of this chapter.

It is possible to look at Oryoki like this. Oryoki itself is the outer form, connected with body. It was developed in Japan to help with practice that embodies the specific points of renunciation, generosity, and meditation in action. The Tibetan monastic meal liturgy is the inner form, connected with speech. It was developed in India or Tibet for the same purpose. The state of mind you have while doing the practice is the secret form, connected with mind. It is the real place and time of all practice and the inner and outer circumstances of speech and body respectively arise from it.

One point that comes from this is that the practice of Oryoki need not be dependent on having a specific, outer circumstance. In Shambhala culture, seminary, dathun, and the like, which are the formal teaching and practice venues of the community, are the official occasions for doing Oryoki. However, if you have confidence in your own mind as mentioned above, you can be less dependent on and even go beyond these formal venues.

The Vidyadhara Chogyam Trungpa strongly urged all of us at the 1982 and 1983 seminaries to incorporate Oryoki into our lives once we had returned home from the seminary. On the face of it, that is not an easy thing to do; Oryoki as most people in Shambhala community experience it is a massive operation and the thought of doing it at home or even in a small group seems impossible. However, that sort of thinking is the style of putting the form first. In fact, Oryoki is a state of mind that brings the outer form. Following on from that, if you put the mind first, then you can easily scale the outer form and the liturgy or modify it so that Oryoki can be managed anytime, anywhere.

The whole thrust of Buddhism is to get out of regimentation, into the openness of realization. From that openness, you provide as much or as little form as is appropriate or even possible on any given occasion. In Vajradhatu, in the early 1980's we developed little black-enamelled tables for doing Oryoki but you could do something else. And food delivery can be made quite easy, even in a small group of people doing it at home. The mechanics can easily be modified to make it work wherever you are.

When you really understand the practice mind of Oryoki, you do not even need the outer form, *per se*. The outer form is intended to help the realization, not hinder it. The liturgy can also be done away with and you can eat a perfect meal of Oryoki without anyone being the wiser. Of course, these comments should not be taken as an excuse for laziness, which is always the danger in presenting a higher level approach.

Altogether, there are many possibilities. For example, I have incorporated the liturgy and a few key parts of the offering process—bowls for offerings for the higher and lower beings—into the main meal taken every day at my home, with my students, family, and other guests who might be there. We sit, Asian-style, at a low table as a matter of course, which does make it easier—because of the key points of the human body—to keep a concentrated state of mind. We have no special tables, gaṇḍhis, or the like and especially, we do not even use Oryoki sets. The meal is served by the cook on a nicely set table, using proper crockery and utensils. We use the liturgy presented in this book, which is easy to do and barely takes time. Sometimes we leave out the recitation of the sutra, if we need to be a little quicker about the meal or if we have guests for whom it would not be fitting. We do the rest of the liturgy always. Everyone works on their own outer form according to the instructions given to them on how to practice mindfulness, alertness[8], and vipashyana while eating. Guests who know none of this join in or not, as they see fit. Those who do wish to join in but who

[8] Mindfulness and alertness are the two key states of mind needed for the development of shamatha.

do not know the outer form are easily able to work with what we provide and the explanation of the offerings only takes a moment. Despite this departure from much of the outer form, we do turn every meal, quite successfully, into the practice that the outer form of Oryoki is intended to support. In this way, with a greater or lesser amount of outer and inner supports, we always do the practice of Oryoki with every midday meal and include all of our guests as well. It is noteworthy that our guests are often very pleased with what they get out of it.

In teaching sessions, we go back to a more complete style of Oryoki though we do not use the black tables and so on but use what makes sense locally. The formality is maintained but with the openness of mind mentioned earlier that can be the starting point, rather than the endpoint, of practice.

This is something that the Vidyadhara wanted. In the days after the seminaries mentioned just above, my friends and I would get together and do Oryoki usually at night after work. We would decide on a menu and divide the tasks of purchasing food, cooking it, and so on. Our meals would usually be followed by sake and discussions relevant to our practice level. It was always very enjoyable and the more so for the fact that we were actually doing what the Vidyadhara had asked of us.

I don't think any of us involved would say that this was "easy". After a day at work, it takes some commitment to come home or go to another place even and put everything together and go through an Oryoki meal. However, it always has, in my experience, the desired effect, that yet another time of eating is turned into a practice session. And more than that, once you have gotten that far, it is easy to continue on from the meal into whatever level of dharma study, celebration, or what have you, that you would like to engage in.

In those years mentioned, I was head of practice at Marpa House and Ani Pema Chodron was one of the residents. She asked me to make sure that there was an Oryoki meal every weekend at the house. As I knew myself from being at the seminaries where the Vidyadhara expressed his wish that Oryoki would be carried into the general life of the practitioners in his community, this was something that should be done. Ani Pema mentioned that the Vidyadhara had encouraged her to do it at Marpa House and other places as part of the more regular flow of life and not just as something reserved for large practice gatherings of seminary, and so on. Again, we had to modify things here and there to make it all work but we did do Oryoki successfully each weekend.

When you understand it like that, you can understand that so-called "Oryoki" can be stripped of the Japanese form and even the liturgy, though that is much harder. You can have a meal—any meal—anywhere and have it be Oryoki. I have found that making the liturgy more important than the outer form provides a way to incorporate the real practice of Oryoki into day to day life easily and in a way that works with little extra effort. That is another reason, apart from the wish to emphasize the oral tradition for the outer form, why this book focusses on giving a very clear explanation of the meal liturgy and does not go into explanations of the outer form.

It would be a mistake to construe the comments in this chapter to mean that the author secretly dislikes the outer form called "Oryoki" and is trying to reduce its significance. That's not the case at all. I truly enjoy doing the full form and fully encourage everyone to learn it and learn it well. Having gone to all that trouble of learning it well, it would be shame to lose the practice totally just because of thinking that the outer form was too cumbersome to fit into daily life.

I do not believe that the Vidyadhara's injunction to take Oryoki into the community's day to day life meant that we slavishly had to do the practice in its most elaborate form. As with so many things that he did, I feel confident that he was directing us to learn the form—outer, inner, and secret—and then work it over so that it would fit and become part of our practice lives. I am happy to report to you that my household has, as outlined above, been able to do that and for the considerable benefit of everyone involved, even for guests who are there just for the one meal. And, as mentioned earlier, I am happy to report that Oryoki has caught people's eye in communities other than Shambhala, and that I feel confident that it can be successfully transplanted there *including* whatever changes might be needed.

The Liturgy

The Sutra of the Recollection of the Noble Three Jewels

I prostrate to the All-Knowing One.

Thus, the buddha bhagavat tathāgata arhat saṃyaksaṃbuddha, possessor of insight and its feet, the sugata, knower of the world, driver who tames beings, unsurpassed, teacher of devas and men, is the buddha bhagavat. That tathāgata corresponds to a cause of merits. His roots of virtue do not go to waste. He is fully ornamented with all patience. His basis is troves of merit. The excellent minor signs adorn him. The flowers of the major marks bloom on him. Perceiving his activity, it being just right, there is harmony. Seeing him, there is no disharmony. He brings true joy to those who long through faith. His prajñā cannot be overpowered. His strengths cannot be challenged. He is the teacher of all sentient beings. He is the father of bodhisatvas. He is the king of noble persons. He is the captain of those who journey to the city of nirvana. His wisdom is unfathomable. His confidence is inconceivable. His speech is complete purity. His melody is pleasing. One never has enough of viewing the image of his body. His body is unparalleled. He is not contaminated by the things of desire. He is very much not contaminated by the things of form. He is not mixed with the things of formlessness. He is completely liberated from the sufferings. He is utterly completely liberated from the skandhas. He does not possess dhātus. His āyatanas are restrained. He has totally cut the knots. He is completely liberated from the torments. He is liberated from craving. He has crossed over the river. His wisdom is totally complete. He abides in the wisdom of the buddha bhagavats who arise in the past, present, and future. He does not abide in nirvana. He abides in the limit of the authentic itself. He abides on the level of looking upon all sentient beings. These are the true qualities of the greatness of the body of the buddha bhagavat.

The holy dharma is good in the beginning, good in the middle, and good at the end. Its meaning is excellent, its wording is excellent. It is not adulterated, is totally complete, is total purity, is total purification. The bhagavat has taught the dharma well. It is authentic sight. It is free from sickness. Its time has no interruption. It brings one in. Seeing it is meaningful. It is known to the wise through individual self-knowing. The dharma taught by the bhagavat is properly revealed in the Vinaya. It is renunciation. It causes one to arrive at complete enlightenment. It is without disharmony and does have inclusion. It has reliability. It does end the journey.

As for the sangha of the great vehicle, they have entered into good, have entered into insight, have entered into straightness, have entered into harmony. They are worthy of joined palms, they are worthy of prostration. They are a field of the glory of merit. They are great ones thoroughly trained in gifts. They are a place for generosity. They are in all places even a great place for generosity.

The protector who possesses great kindness,
The all-knowing teacher,
The basis of oceans of merit and virtue,
I prostrate to the tathāgata.

Pure, the cause of freedom from passion,
Virtuous, liberating from the lower realms,
This alone is the supreme, ultimate truth:
I prostrate to the dharma, which is peace.

Having been liberated, they show the path to
  liberation;
They are fully dedicated to the disciplines;
They are a holy field of merit and possess virtue:
I prostrate to the saṅgha.

I prostrate to the Buddha, the leader;
I prostrate to the dharma, the protector;
I prostrate to the saṅgha, the community:
I prostrate respectfully and always to these three.

The Buddha's virtues are inconceivable;
The dharma's virtues are inconceivable;
The saṅgha's virtues are inconceivable;
Having faith in these inconceivables,
Therefore, the fruitions are inconceivable:
May I be born in a completely pure realm.

Substances that have been offered to the Three Jewels
  and plunder from others—

I have completely abandoned all such impure and perverted nourishment;
This food is in accord with the dharma, free from evil deeds:
May the health of my body flourish.

Then bless the food with:

OṂ ĀḤ HŪṂ

From the "Lamp on Summed Up Conduct":

Divide the food into four parts.
First, offer pure food to the devas.
After that, to the dharmapālas and protectors
Offer elaborate torma.
Then, eat and drink.
Give the leftover, to all the bhūtas.

In that way, or else, as is said in the Vinaya of the holy dharma, divide the food into three parts. First, offer divine food to the gurus with:

OṂ GURU-VAJRA-NAIVEDYĀ ĀḤ HŪṂ

Likewise, offer to the host of buddha, and bodhisatvas with:

OM SARVA-BUDDHA-BODHISATVEBHYO VAJRA-NAIVEDYĀ ĀḤ HŪṂ

Offer to the divine assembly of the maṇḍala of yidams with:

OṂ KĀMA-DEVA-MAṆḌALA-NAIVEDYĀ ĀḤ HŪṂ

Offer to Mañjuśhrī and others—whatever devata you desire—for example:

OṂ MAÑJUŚHRĪ VAJRA-NAIVEDYĀ ĀḤ HŪṂ

Offer to the dharmapālas with:

OṂ ŚHRĪ DHARMAPĀLA VAJRA-NAIVEDYĀ ĀḤ HŪṂ

Offer divine food to all the bhūtas with:

OṂ A-KĀRO MUKHAṂ SARVA-DHARMĀṆĀṂ ĀDYANUTPANNATVĀT OṂ ĀḤ HŪṂ PHAṬ SVĀHĀ

Give one pinch of food to Hārītī with:

OṂ HĀRĪTE SVĀHĀ

and one pinch of food to the five hundred sons of Hārītī with:

OṂ HĀRĪTE MAHĀYAKṢHIṆĪ HARA HARA SARVA-RĀYAṆIKṢHIṂ SVĀHĀ

Give one pinch of food to the bhūtas who are capable of receiving the select portion with:

OṂ AGRA-PIṆḌA-ĀŚHIBHYAḤ SVĀHĀ

If one wishes to purify any poison or the like in the food, chant:

NAMAḤ SARVA-BUDDHA-BODHISATVĀNĀṂ OṂ BALIṂ TE JVĀLA-BALIṂ NI SVĀHĀ

Repeat this eight times; pick up food with the thumb and ring fingers, and eat.

While eating, eat with an attitude that sees the food as impure, with an attitude of non-attachment, with an attitude that benefits the masses of different intestinal bacteria, and with an attitude of remaining on the ship that travels to peace and enlightenment. Do not eat with an attitude that increases passion and craving. In "Entrance to the Bodhisatva's Conduct" it is said, "One should eat moderately." The way of doing this is explained according to the "Ashtanga": "Two quarters of the stomach are for food; one quarter is for drink, and one quarter is left empty." Or else, according to the text "Handbook of Food": "One should have two-thirds for food and drink, and leave one-third empty." Finally, give a pinch of food to the bhutas who are capable of receiving the leftovers with:

OṂ UCCHIṢHṬA-PIṆḌA-ĀŚHIBHYAḤ SVĀHĀ

Then, wash the mouth. Then, purify the gift:

I prostrate to the bhagavat, tathāgata, arhat,
saṃyaksaṃbuddha Samantaprabharaja:

NAMAḤ SAMANTAPRABHĀRĀJĀYA TATHĀGATĀYA
ARHATE SAṂYAKSAṂBUDDHĀYA / NAMO MAÑJUŚHRĪ
KUMĀRABHŪTĀYA BODHISATVĀYA MAHĀSATTVĀYA
MAHĀKĀRUNIKĀYA / TAD YATHĀ / OṂ NIRĀLAMBE
NIRĀBHASE JAYA JAYA LABHE MAHĀMATE DAKṢHE
DAKṢHIṆI ME PARIŚHODHĀYA SVĀHĀ

By saying this dharaṇi even once, one completely purifies alms as vast as Mount Meru. This dharaṇi is taken from the "Dulwa Nampar Ngepe Gyu". Then, as is said in the āgamas:

May the royal patron and likewise
The other sentient beings who are donors
Obtain long life, freedom from sickness, prosperity,
And the companionship of eternal bliss.

That and:

By this generosity one has power over the bhūtas.
By this generosity one is free from enemies.
Generosity is the transcendent friend.
Therefore, generosity is said to be essential.

Generosity is the ornament of the world.
Through generosity, one turns back from the lower realms.
Generosity is the stairway to the higher realms.
Generosity is the virtue that produces peace.

The prosperity of the bodhisatvas
Is inexhaustible, filling the whole of space.
In order to obtain such prosperity,
Completely propagate that generosity.

Say these verses of dedication, aspiration, and generosity.

Also, those who, having the yoga of a deity, would like to make eating into the revelry of the inner gaṇachakra, can use OṂ ĀḤ HŪṂ *to make the food blaze forth as oceans of cloudbanks of desirables the nature of amṛita then say,*

HOḤ
My body of skandhas, dhātus, and āyatanas
In fact the complete three seats is
The deities of the maṇḍalas of the hundred holy families
Whose every movement is greater bliss
Playing in the unsurpassed vajra samaya
In a great cloud of bodhicitta
In the state of non-duality's equality.

The path substances have been fulfilled with the yoga
So there will be no obscuration due to food;
There's no particular sponsor here but
May they live in the fruition of the Great Vehicle.

Use the technique of offering with your skandhas, dhātus, and āyatanas visualized as the complete three seats to discard clinging to ordinary appearances and enjoy yourself with satisfaction. Having done so, say this:

Having turned the wheel of feast
In the maṇḍala of the complete three seats
May I and others, all migrators without exception,
Gain accomplishment in the same maṇḍala.

This comes from the Tārā Essence, and is an inner feast offering of the Anuyoga system.

Complete Explanation of the Liturgy

1. Recollection of the Noble Three Jewels and Taking Refuge in Them

The liturgy starts with the recitation of a sutra for the purpose of bringing the good qualities of the Three Jewels clearly to mind and that is followed by several verses that further remember the qualities of the Three Jewels and take refuge in them.

One of the very early teachings given by the Buddha was called "The Six Recollections". The purpose of the Six Recollections is to arouse and deepen faith. It is a Lesser Vehicle teaching but, because it is so fundamental to all levels of practice, it is regarded as a universal teaching good for all Buddhists. Therefore, the same six recollections are also found in the Great Vehicle.

The text of the six recollections can be found in the Pali Canon or you can read all six together with what is regarded as the standard, Theravada commentary on their use in *The Path Of Purification*[9]. The text of the Six Recol-

---

[9] "Visuddhimagga" by Bhadantācariya Buddhaghosa, translated from the Pali by Bhikkhu Ñāṇamoli as "The Path Of Purification", published by the Buddhist Publication Society, Kandy, Shri Lanka.

lections was also available in Sanskrit as part of the Great Vehicle Canon.

The first three recollections are about Buddha, Dharma, and Sangha and are called "Recollection of the Buddha", "Recollection of the Dharma", and "Recollection of the Sangha" respectively. These recollections are very short: the one for the Buddha lists nine qualities, the one for the Dharma lists six qualities, and the one for the Sangha lists nine qualities. The followers of the Great Vehicle extended these listings by adding more qualities for each. The extended versions were called "The Sutra of the Recollection of the Buddha", "The Sutra of the Recollection of the Dharma", and "The Sutra of the Recollection of the Sangha" respectively. The three sutras were translated from Sanskrit and included in the Tibetan Canon in the *Translations of the Buddha Word*[10]. These three small sutras were combined into one larger one for ease of use which was then called *The Sutra of the Recollection of the Noble Three Jewels.* This is the sutra that the meal liturgy starts with. Essentially speaking, it is a development of the first three of the Lesser Vehicle's Six Recollections that the Buddha recommended for the use of all his disciples as the way to arouse and deepen faith.

One key point about *The Sutra of the Recollection of the Noble Three Jewels* is that, although it is a Great Vehicle development of a Lesser Vehicle teaching, it has not had anything that is specific to the Great Vehicle added to it, rather, the additions all stay within the Lesser Vehicle

---

[10] Tib. bka' bsgyur. Phonetically, "kangyur". The Tibetan Canon of the words of the Buddha.

theme and style of the original teaching. For example, when the dharma is typified, it is not typified as teaching on emptiness, great compassion, or other themes specific to the Great Vehicle but is typified as "renunciation" which is one of the central themes of the Lesser Vehicle. That is important to understanding the role that the Vidyadhara wanted for the practise of Oryoki and the use of the meal liturgy in Shambhala culture. One way to see it is that this was his way of introducing the teaching of the Six Recollections to his sangha.

There are a number of commentaries authored by Tibetans on the meaning of the *Sutra* itself[11]. For Kagyu and Nyingma followers two are notable; one by the great master of the Jonang tradition, Taranatha, and one by the great Nyingma scholar Ju Mipham[12].

The combined sutra is the first thing that the Vidyadhara taught when he began his teaching career at an early age. Later, in the West, the Vidyadhara used the sutra as the

---

[11] These commentaries only explain the combined sutra, which is the first section of the liturgy, the paragraphs that extol the qualities of the buddha, dharma, and sangha. The commentaries stop there and do not mention the rest of the liturgy.

[12] Ju Mipham was a very great Rimey scholar of the nineteenth century, a contemporary of Kongtrul the Great and Khyentse the Great. I refer to him here as Ju Mipham, which was his usual name, to avoid any confusion between him and other persons named Mipham. In Tibetan culture, people were often called their personal name with the place they came from before it. Mipham was from Ju, so, of many Miphams, he was the one from Ju.

basis for his talks in the Hinayana section of the 1982 seminary. By doing so, he explained the meaning of buddha, dharma, and sangha to the seminary participants and at the same time gave impetus to the practice of Oryoki within the community, a practice which had only been in place for a couple of years. The Vidyadhara explained the sutra always using the commentary by Ju Mipham.

As mentioned in the general introduction, it heard those seminary talks, based on Ju Mipham's commentary, from the Vidyadhara in person. Later, I also received a complete teaching on Ju Mipham's commentary from Khenpo Padma Tshewang, the Head Khenpo of Shri Singha Institute, the exceptionally famous Buddhist College of Dzogchen Monastery in Tibet. Thus, I used the same commentary as the Vidyadhara, and with a full transmission of the meaning from these two masters, to translate and compose an explanation of the sutra.

I started out by using the Nalanda Translation Committee's original translation of the sutra which still appears in the Oryoki liturgy at the time of writing. Unfortunately, and as can be clearly seen from Mipham's commentary and all the explanations I have had of it, there are a significant number of errors in that translation, so many that a re-translation was unavoidable. The new translation is used throughout and the explanation of the sutra follows that translation. The explanation of the sutra has the words of the sutra set off in italics so that they can easily be distinguished within the explanation. A full translation of Ju Mipham's commentary to the sutra and extensive writings on the sutra and the use of it to develop faith, renunciation is available in a separate publication from Padma Karpo Translation Committee called "Unending Auspiciousness".

❁ ❁ ❁

Complete Explanation of the *Sutra of the Recollection of the Noble Three Jewels*

i. The Title

The title of the sutra is *The Sutra of the Recollection of the Three Noble Jewels*. The translation of the meal liturgy made by Nalanda Translation Committee makes it seem as though the title of the whole liturgy is *The Sutra of the Recollection of the Three Noble Jewels* when in fact the liturgy has no title but begins by mentioning the name of the sutra which is the first thing to be recited in the liturgy.

ii. The Translator's Homage

I prostrate to the All-Knowing One is the translator's homage of the sutra. There was a great revision in the ninth century A.D. of the translations of Buddhist works that had already been made into the Tibetan language. To go with it, the king of the time, Tri Ralpachen, declared that there would be a standard form of homage included in all translations. A text connected with the Vinaya was to have the wording "I prostrate to the All-Knowing One" for the homage. Thus, the homage here tells us that this is a sutra connected with the Vinaya section of the teachings of the Buddha. That sets the tone for the whole of what follows. Here "the All-Knowing One" means "the buddha, the one who has that kind of knowledge that sees all phenomena in both their depth and extent". You might wonder, "Why isn't this "the omniscient one"?" A distinction is made between his quality as all-knowing and omniscient in the sutras. Here, the name says "all-knowing one", not omniscient one, and it means the one who sees all things that are knowable.

iii. The Text Itself

Following the homage, there is the actual text of the sutra, which is in three sections, one for the recollection of each of the Three Jewels. Each section comes out as one paragraph in the translation—the first for the recollection of the qualities of buddha, the second for the recollection of the qualities of the dharma, and the third for the recollection of the qualities of the sangha. A full explanation of each section follows.

In a session of Oryoki practice, the entire sutra, starting with the homage, is to be recited once. During the time that it is being recited, the Oryoki set is opened according to the Japanese form for doing so.

A. The Qualities of Buddha

The good qualities of the Buddha are given in three parts. First there is a summary of the good qualities of the Buddha. Second there is an extensive explanation of both the causes and the fruitions involved in buddhahood. Third is a conclusion.

The first part is contained in the first sentence, ***thus, the Buddha, bhagavat... is the buddha bhagavat***. It sums up the qualities of the Buddha by listing a number of his main epithets. The epithets in this first sentence are a group of epithets have traditionally been repeated as a formula in Buddhist cultures. This summary of the Buddha's qualities has been recited day in and out in every Buddhist culture from the time of the Buddha. It is very well known and loved.

Buddha had an enormous number of epithets given to him while he was alive and a large number of these became incorporated into the Buddhist tradition. Each one has much meaning in terms of pointing out what a buddha is but more than that, these epithets have for thousands of years evoked a great deal of faith in the Buddha whenever they have been repeated.

That then is the point here; as you recite the words, they remind you of what a buddha is which becomes a way of arousing faith in the Buddha. The same is true for the sections on dharma and sangha. Altogether, recitation of the sutra is meant to lead to a deepening of understanding of the Three Jewels which in turn is meant to lead to a mind that takes refuge in them.

Buddha means "enlightened one". This is sometimes translated into English as "awakened one" because of following the Tibetan reasoning for their translation of "buddha" from Sanskrit. However, the original Sanskrit conveys the sense of a person who is illuminated with knowledge and the term "enlightened one" is closest to it. The Sanskrit word "bodhi" most commonly translated as "enlightenment" is almost the same as the word "buddha", with both of them coming from the same root that has the sense of illumination. Thus, when we say something like, "The enlightened one is enlightened", in English, it has exactly the same feel as when the same thing was said in the language of ancient India.

As a matter of interest, this highlights one of the great difficulties of translating Buddhist teaching from Tibetan into English. Tibetans often created new words in their language as they attempted to get the meaning of the Sanskrit into Tibetan and then produced explanations of the new words and why they were fitting. However, the explanations are specific to the Tibetan context and sometimes are not suitable for English or another language context. For example, "buddha" was translated into Tibetan with two words put together, meaning "awakened and blossomed". The rationale behind the translation is very fine, being based on an important phrase in Buddhist culture that was in use from the time of the Buddha. Nonetheless, when the original Sanskrit is looked at, it turns out that there is another wording even closer to the meaning of "buddha" than the phrase meaning "awakened and blossomed" that the Tibetans used as the basis for their translation. That other wording means "realization" or "knowledge" and does not convey the sense of "awakening" but conveys the sense of "becoming enlightened". The Tibetan translators were very knowledgeable and did an excellent job when they did their work of translating "buddha" into the Tibetan language context. However, the English situation is different. To begin with, unlike the Tibetan language at the time of that translation, English already has a specific term that is very close to the meaning of "buddha". Therefore, the rationale used by the Tibetans for their translation of "buddha", while helpful in terms of understanding what a buddha is, does not apply to the task of translating "buddha" into English. The English "enlightened one" is actually a much closer translation of the Sanskrit word "buddha" than the word invented by the Tibetans "awakened and blossomed one".

This highlights a specific problem that comes for us non-Tibetans wanting to translate Buddhism into our own languages. If we use the Tibetan Buddhist language as a basis for translation, we are translating from a language which is already a translation. It is well-known in all fields of translation, not just Buddhist ones, that translating from something that is already a translation is not nearly as good as translating from the original language. This problem is seen very clearly in a number of places in this sutra, not only with this word "buddha" found right at its beginning.

The English language is much closer linguistically to Sanskrit than is Tibetan. Thus it often happens that Buddhist words to be translated into English go very nicely directly from the Sanskrit, without having to face the difficulties of translating from the Tibetan, itself already a translation. The example above is a perfect example of this: the Tibetans were not able to translate either the word "bodhi" or the word "buddha" directly and literally into their language but had to resort to producing a new word in each case. The Tibetan words do not translate well into English, as one might expect since one is doing a translation of a translation. However, the original Sanskrit words do translate very nicely, almost perfectly in fact, into English with "enlightened one" and "enlightenment" as just described. In short, the "Buddha" is the "enlightened one".

Bhagavat is an ancient Indian term which is used as a term of high respect for someone who is considered to possess a great degree of holiness. The word bhagavat was and still is used by many Indian spiritual traditions as a term of the highest respect for the holy beings of their system and this is how the term should be understood here. The translation "blessed one" captures the original meaning of bhagavat well and has been used for example by the Nalanda Translation Committee in their translation of the *Prajñāpāramitā Heart Sutra*.

When the Tibetans translated "bhagavat" into their own language, they started with the exact and literal translation of the Sanskrit, which is "chom den". However, the early translators said that this was not enough because "chom den" could refer to a holy person in any religious group, not just to a buddha. They wanted it to refer only to a buddha so they added an extra word to the end of "chom den" to give it their desired, extra meaning. Their new term, "chom den day[13]", was a description of a *buddha* type of bhagavat in particular. This new term for bhagavat made from the three, distinct terms—chom, den, and day—was explained by the early translators to mean, "he who has conquered the māras; he who has come to possesses the two accumulations; and he who has transcended the two obscurations". Note the last one, which is the special piece they added. Only a buddha has transcended the two obscurations, thus the Tibetan translation of bhagavat is not really a translation of the original word but is a modification of the original so that it only refers to a *buddha* bhagavat.

Now, rather than assume the special meaning given by the Tibetans, you might do better to understand it according to the original meaning of a holy person that was in use at the buddha's time. There is nothing lost in doing this because the sutra itself does not just say "bhagavat" which could be any holy person of any religious tradition but says "buddha bhagavat" which tells you specifically which kind of holy being you are talking about. For myself, I find that understanding things this way actually brings a sense of the situation as it was in India and this only furthers my faith, which is the intended purpose. You might be able to find the same, too.

Tathāgata translates as "one who has gone—gata—to suchness—tathā". It means someone who has attained enlightenment by having journeyed back to suchness, meaning reality.

---

[13] Tib. bcom ldan 'das.

Arhat is derived from the Sanskrit "arhan" meaning "to be worthy of praise" or "venerable". Again, the Tibetans did not translate it literally but made a new word to give a desired, specific meaning. Their new word "dra chom pa[14]" means "one who has destroyed the enemy". The Tibetans then explained that an arhat in the Buddhist tradition is someone who has defeated the principal enemy of sentient beings, the afflictions[15]. They explained that such a person has extricated himself from samsara and become noble, spiritually speaking, compared to those who are still in samsara. His higher position makes him worthy of respect and that is why he was called an arhat in ancient India. Again we see that, if we translate from the Tibetan translation, it leads us to what has become the popular English translation, "foe destroyer". However, the Sanskrit does not mean that and we could find a word that simply and correctly translates the actual meaning of the word. At the same time, a study of the Tibetan rationale in conjunction with a study of the original term can lead to a very good understanding of the meaning of the word, as can be in these cases here.

Some people become confused at this point, because of thinking that "arhat" is a special name only used for those who have attained the fruition of the Lesser Vehicle. They cannot see how the tathāgata could be an arhat because an arhat has a lesser level of realization than a tathāgata. However, there are other ways of using the

---

[14] Tib. dgra bcom pa.

[15] Skt. kleśha. This is often translated as "emotions" but Buddha specifically used the word kleśha which means "an affliction".

word "arhat". Here it does not mean that the Buddha is a Lesser Vehicle arhat with a lower level of attainment. Rather, it points out that one facet of the Buddha is that he also has an arhat's level of attainment. In other words, a buddha's attainment is so complete that it includes everything attained by the arhats of the Lesser Vehicle.

The Buddha was not merely an arhat of the Lesser Vehicle. He was much more than that. He was a ***saṃyak saṃbuddha*** meaning a "true, complete buddha". In the ancient tradition of Buddhism, beings who had gone to the end of the Lesser Vehicle were called "buddha"; they were the shravakabuddhas and pratyekabuddhas who were the arhats of the Lesser Vehicle. They were also called "arhat buddhas" which might seem strange if you have not heard it before but it is part of the tradition; it is like saying in English "the enlightened type of person called an arhat". Then there were the bodhisatva[16] buddhas, the ones who have been through the bodhisatva journey and attained the highest possible level of buddhahood. The bodhisatva buddhas were not merely arhats with their partial enlightenment but were ***samyak sambuddhas*** meaning "true, complete buddhas" ones who really were buddhas with the most complete type of enlightenment possible. Therefore, the Buddha himself coined the term "true, complete buddha" to indicate a person who has gone through the Great Vehicle journey and attained an enlightenment which is truly—that is to say really and truly—complete. Thus, the Buddha has all

[16] This is the correct spelling according to the Tibetan traditions and the Indians who assisted the original Tibetan translators so it is followed here.

of the qualities of an arhat buddha but is also a truly complete buddha.

Possessor of insight and its feet. The literal translation of the original Sanskrit phrase is "possessor of insight and what comes at foot". Furthermore, the "what comes at foot" actually has the sense of "what carries the insight around". The phrase was occasionally used in ancient India for the worldly, general meaning of "someone who has intelligence and good character with it". Because of that, Nalanda Translation Committee translated it as "learned and virtuous" but that is not the meaning here. The meaning here is "the one who possesses insight and also the various qualities that go with and serve it, like feet that carry it along".

The key quality of a Buddha is insight and that is the key quality that has to be developed on the path. The other qualities of enlightenment are needed but, in the Buddhist way, these all come below and serve the insight. On the path, one needs insight and the other qualities that serve it in order to go to enlightenment, and, once one has attained enlightenment, the insight together with all the other qualities that go with it that one has are now used to serve sentient beings. Thus this phrase refers to something that is true both on the journey to enlightenment and at the time of enlightenment. Ju Mipham gives in his commentary the example of a person walking along a road: the eyes see the place to be travelled and the feet below it make the journey, similarly, insight sees the way and the other qualities that it has below it serve to carry the person along.

The sugata. The Sanskrit word has two parts: "su" means any kind of happy, easy, pleasant situation and "gata" is the same as in "tathāgata" and means "gone" or "is going". Thus the term can mean either "someone who has gone to happiness", that is, someone who has gone to the blissful state of liberation or "someone who has gone happily, easily, pleasantly", that is, someone who has gone on a path that was easy and pleasant to travel. The first meaning points out the kind of fruition that a person goes to using the Buddhist path; this is the kind of fruition that the Buddha has obtained. The second meaning points out the kind of path that the Buddhist path is; it is a straightforward one that leads where it is supposed to, without twists, so it is easy, and it is a pleasant one because it passes through all the happy, pleasant, and even blissful states of mind on its way.

This term is similar to tathāgata but has a less philosophical quality to it; it has a very practical sense of "someone who has progressed along the Buddhist path, a path that is fundamentally workable, and has therefore gone easily to the great state of ease through practice".

In general, practitioners of the Great Vehicle work towards buddhahood with two aims in mind; they plan to solve their own problems by becoming a buddha and, equally, they plan to bring others to the same place so as to solve their problems, too. In this sense, buddhahood is attainment of the complete purity of mind called the dharmakāya and the two complete purities of body called saṃbhogakāya and nirmāṇakāya. Attainment of the first fulfills one's own aims or purposes because it brings personal, final release from all problems. The second fulfills others' aims or purposes because it works to bring all other sentient beings to their own, final release from all problems. If you stop and think about it, you will see that, up to this point, the epithets all point at qualities that a buddha has developed for his own purposes. Now, the remainder of this formula mentions qualities that are possessed because of fulfilling others' purposes.

The Buddha was referred to at one point in his career out of awe of his capabilities as the one who knows everything about the worlds and all of the beings in them. This succinct estimation of his capabilities became, after the ones just mentioned, one of his main epithets. A buddha knows everything about the world, the beings in it, and the miseries and otherwise of those beings. Note that "world" here does not just mean this world but means "worlds in general". The Buddha knows all beings everywhere and all of their situations, in all of the worlds, physical and otherwise, and knows all of that always and in every moment. Because of that knowledge, he can and does do whatever needs to be done to benefit the beings of those worlds. Thus he is ***the knower of the world*** and it should be understood that "world" here refers to the entirety of all worlds and all of their differing situations.

In general, a buddha steers beings away from samsara towards enlightenment. To get them to enlightenment, he has to tame them. Because he knows the minds of all beings—whether they are hard to tame because of having a tough character or easy to tame because of having been on the path for some time already—he also knows exactly which methods to use to tame them. No one else matches his capacities for steering and taming beings, thus he is unsurpassed by any other in this regard. Therefore, he is ***the driver who is the tamer of beings, the unsurpassed one.***

The word driver here is a generic term used to mean anyone in control of any vehicle, animal, or situation. It has the sense of the person at the helm, the steersman. In ancient India it would have been used to refer to the driver of a chariot but not only that, to elephant drivers, and horsemen, and so on—anyone in the driver's seat. In this case, the Buddha is the driver who steers beings away from samsara and towards enlightenment, thus, he is not just any driver but is specifically the sort of driver who is the tamer of beings. No-one else can match a buddha's capabilities when it comes to taming beings primarily because he pervades all situations and knows them exactly as they are. As a true buddha with everything implied by that, he has skills as a teacher that cannot be matched. For that reason, buddhas in general are unsurpassed in their capacity as the drivers who tame beings. Note how "unsurpassed" is a separate item but goes with the "driver who is the tamer of beings" and not as a separate item. There is a difficulty here which is that some editions of the liturgy have the "unsurpassed" joined into the "driver who is the tamer of beings" and others have it immediately following. The commentaries make it clear that these are two separate items but go together as one item, as has been translated and explained here.

How did this unsurpassed driver who tames beings actually go about taming the beings? The Buddha did not merely manifest as a buddha in the world of humans but manifested his enlightenment cosmically, throughout all the places of beings of all times. Only beings in certain places had the capacity to hear, contemplate, and cultivate the dharma of a buddha by receiving the dharma directly from him or one of his followers. Those places were certain heavens of the devas—some in the high levels of the desire realm and some in the lower levels of the form realm—and human realms. Therefore, his enlightenment manifested cosmically but it was specifically in the worlds of devas and humans that he became a wheel-turning buddha who taught the beings there. Here, "teacher" does not mean any teacher but is the term used for a person who founds and is the proclaimer within the world of a whole system of dharma. The Buddha aided many beings in many ways but, specifically, he was the founding teacher who showed the teachings of a buddha to devas and humans, both. Thus it says, ***the teacher of devas and men***.

Such are the qualities of the buddha as expressed through the principal epithets that were used to describe him in ancient India so this summary concludes with ***is the buddha bhagavat***. You could review the explanation of the words "buddha" and "bhagavat" at the beginning of this section to remind yourself of the meaning of the words.

That completes the first part, the summary in formula form of the Buddha's qualities—both those connected with the achievement of his own purposes and those connected with the achievement of others' purposes.

The second part is a more extensive description of the Buddha's qualities. It has two parts. First it sets out how he manifested to fulfill the aims of others, then it sets out how he totally abandoned samsara and realized nirvana to fulfill his own aims.

That tathāgata corresponds to a cause of merits. The text does not say "the tathāgata" but "that tathāgata" where the "that" specifically means "that kind of tathāgata whose qualities have just been mentioned in brief". Everything about the tathāgata is related to the accumulation of merit. As a tathāgata, he is the result of an immeasurable merit collection accumulated over cosmic ages.

His roots of virtue do not go to waste. In general, virtuous action produces roots of virtue. "Root" has the specific sense of a karmic seed that could come into effect and produce something virtuous. It conveys the idea of the possibility of production of virtue at a later time. While he was on the path, the Buddha did not waste his roots of virtue by using them for good results within samsara nor did he allow them to go to waste by becoming a Lesser Vehicle arhat. He used his roots of virtue entirely for the cause of truly complete enlightenment. On top of that, after attaining buddhahood, his roots of merit are never used in a way that would allow them to go to waste. Instead, they are a cause of unending goodness both for himself and all beings. On becoming a buddha, the roots of virtue that he had accumulated became part of the pool of virtue of a buddha, which is an unending situation. Thus, even though his roots of virtue as a buddha are used for the production of goodness, his use of them never exhausts them and hence they never go to waste by his use of them. In other words, he has achieved an accumulation of merit that unendingly produces good and hence never goes to an end.

He is fully ornamented with all patience. The Buddha practised all of the different types of patience on his way to buddhahood and,in doing so, perfected patience in its totality, meaning in all ways possible. Not only that but, once he had become a buddha, he had types of patience that were consistent with his being beyond ordinary concept. For example, he could sit his body in one place for countless aeons, without moving, if necessary. This kind of patience is beyond the patience practised on the path. The Buddha is fully ornamented with all types of patience, both the different types of patience that can be distinguished on the path to buddhahood and at the fruition of buddhahood.

His basis is troves of merit. Here "trove" means a source that is like a treasure that never ends. The Buddha, as a buddha, comes from merit and not just small amounts of it but an immeasurably large collection of it. Thus, on the one hand, he is a trove of merit that came from his practice of the path. Then, on the other hand, no-one else in the world has shown or does show all the details of what should be rejected and what should be adopted in the course of taming the mind and producing the merit needed for enlightenment. Thus, having become buddha, he is a trove of merit in that he becomes a basis for others' developments of their own troves of merit.

Because the Buddha has perfected his accumulation of merit, he has become a buddha. Signs of his extraordinary accumulations of merit appear on his nirmāṇakāya body as the thirty-two major marks and eight minor signs. Thus, ***the excellent minor signs adorn him*** and ***the flowers of the major marks bloom on him***. In fact, the minor signs or marks as they have often been called are really "the excellent insignia" and the "major marks" as they have been called are really just the "marks". Not only the buddha of our time but all buddhas have these signs and marks present on their nirmāṇakāya bodies. For instance, they have the large protuberance on top of the head, they have dark head hair with each hair individually curled in a particular manner, they have very long earlobes, beautiful eyes, a curled hair between their eyebrows, and so on. You can see these signs in traditional iconographic representations such as statues and paintings. They are listed in a number of Great Vehicle sutras and also are listed in Maitreya's text *The Ornament of Emergent Realisation*[17].

Note that the text does not say that he blooms with the major marks. As Ju Mipham points out in his commentary, the major marks bloom on him and the minor signs are like anthers of those freshly opened flowers that serve to enhance the appearance of the major marks.

---

[17] Skt. Abhisamayālaṅkāra. A translation is contained in Edward Conze's *Sutra of the Perfection of Wisdom* and extensive listings and explanations are given in my own *The Illuminator Tibetan-English Dictionary*.

Perceiving his activity, it being just right, there is harmony. The meaning of the words describing this quality is not obvious in the Tibetan and Tibetan commentaries do have to make some effort to clarify it. This is about the mental perception of a person seeing a buddha. It is paired with the next quality which is similar but about the content of visual appearance. This quality means that anything a buddha does is always done so that it will be just right for the person who is perceiving it. It will be "tailor-made" to fit with the person's constitution, senses, and thoughts. The buddha's activity, when it actually is perceived by a person, that is, when it becomes an object of perception for that person, will only ever be in perfect correspondence, or harmony, with that particular person. The activity has been made "just right" for the mind-stream of that being, so there will only ever be harmony between the activity as perceived and the mind of the being.

Moreover, a buddha's form is perfectly proportioned and has none of the jaggedness that can appear on a human form. For example, his height and width are such that he has perfect symmetry, like the Nyagrodha tree of India whose height and spreading branches have a symmetry perfectly pleasing to the eye. His joints never bulge out and are never angular; his shoulders are perfectly rounded, his knees smooth, his ankle bones not evident, his elbows smooth and rounded, and so on. Therefore, ***seeing him, there is no disharmony*** means that no disharmony of his form is known when he is seen visually.

His beyond-worldly beauty combined with his virtuous presence is such that anyone who goes before him has pure faith arise in the mind just by the power of his presence. That pure faith then leads to the development of such strong interest in him that the person becomes totally absorbed with him, so much so that the person would not notice even if someone beat him while he was watching. Then, that interest, which you could say is a kind of longing, leads to a very pure, overt kind of joy. This sequence of events is summed up in ***he brings true joy to those who long through faith*** though note that the English reverses the sequence. The sutra has this sequence: faith arises in those who come into his presence which leads to intense interest in him which leads to a very pure, overt joy arising in them.

A buddha's wisdom has no obscuration whatsoever to its function of knowing. Therefore it has total knowledge of all things through time and space. Because of that, noone can be a match for a buddha. He cannot be tricked, tripped up, or have anything hidden from him. He is always on top of every situation. Therefore, ***his prajñā cannot be overpowered***. There are many stories in the sutras about this, for example, the stories about his jealous cousin Devadatta who was constantly trying to outdo the Buddha but who could never win because the Buddha's knowledge was always on top of the situation.

A buddha has many qualities of mind and body including many abilities called "strengths". These strengths of a buddha can never be matched. Even if someone were to challenge him to a contest of abilities, the person would not be able to defeat him, let alone match him. Therefore, ***his strengths cannot be challenged***. There are many stories in the sutras about his strengths and challenges to them that he successfully met.

The next four phrases go together, showing how the Buddha leads beings in various ways.

Firstly, overall, the buddha is the teacher of all sentient beings. A buddha has the knowledge and capacity to be the teacher for any and every sentient being. Even if there were a human who could teach everyone in the human world successfully, that person could not teach hell beings and hungry ghosts and so on, let alone gods in the form and formless realms. Unlike ordinary people who usually have limitations on who they can teach or help, a buddha has the capacity to be a teacher for all beings throughout time and space. Therefore, overall, ***he is the teacher of all sentient beings***.

The next three lines show particular ways that he leads beings. His main job is to be father to the bodhisatvas in the Great Vehicle so ***he is the father of bodhisatvas***. He is the father of bodhisatvas and they in turn are the sons of the conquerors. There is a whole vision to the Great Vehicle that is enacted with him as the father and them as the sons. Amongst other things, the Great Vehicle speaks of the sons who hold the family lineage of a buddha and who do the deeds of that family until they have prepared themselves for the final coronation; at that time, their father, their buddha, enthrones and empowers them into buddhahood. As well as that, ***he is the king of noble persons*** meaning that he acts as a king who presides over and leads the arhats of the Lesser Vehicle. He goes with them on their journey and does their Lesser Vehicle things with them so that they can attain the fruition of their particular path.

The last quality raises a really major point for the Shambhala community. The term “noble one” has been widely misunderstood in Shambhala society. At the time of writing I saw, through a whole series of posts to the Shambhala user lists, that it has been mis-used to the point that there is now an entrenched unwillingness even to see the possibility of an error.

The term “noble one” translates the Sanskrit term “ārya”. From the beginning, the Buddha used this term to refer specifically to those persons or principles which are beyond samsara. For example, in the case of the sangha, it does not mean “those fellows of mine in the community whom I think to be wonderful and fine” which is now trenchantly upheld as the meaning. Rather, it specifically refers to those who have attained the path of insight and who therefore have stepped out of samsara and become part of the sangha Jewel in whom we take refuge.

As a matter of interest, when the Vidyadhara was alive, he set down the rule that he was the only one allowed to address the sangha as “the noble sangha”. Somewhere along the line that was lost and it became common to use “the noble sangha” as an address to others in the community with the idea that they are the “very fine members of this Buddhist community”. In doing so, the specific meaning of “noble one” and “noble sangha” as used in Buddhism has been lost. That is a major problem because there is a significant portion of Buddhist understanding that depends on the distinction between a spiritually noble person and a spiritual commoner. For example, the whole understanding of the sangha refuge Jewel depends on that distinction. The sangha that you take refuge in is not the local sangha in your community; they might be fine people but most of them, at least, will be spiritual commoners. The sangha that you take refuge in, which is the meaning of the sangha Jewel, is the noble sangha, and that is the only usage of the words "noble sangha" or "noble ones" found in the Buddhist world.

Accordingly, the text here is specifically saying that the Buddha presides over the noble ones of the Buddhist path, that is, the ones who have gained the attainment of the path of insight, as their king. It is *not* saying that the buddha presides like a king over our sangha of fellow practitioners whom we see as so wonderful.

Then, the Buddha in general is like a captain who actually does the work of taking all like-minded beings from the dank dungeon of samsara to the grand city of nirvana, as it is called in Buddhist parlance. Therefore, ***he is the captain of those who journey to the city of nirvana***. The wording here is very specific. It does not simply mean that he is guiding a group to the city of nirvana. It has the greater meaning that the buddha is at the helm and captains those various people who have undertaken the journey themselves. He not only guides them but actually does all the work, as a captain does, of gathering them up and shepherding them to their destination.

That completes the section on his qualities in terms of fulfilling the aims of others. The rest of the qualities of a buddha mentioned in the sutra concern a buddha's abandonment of samsara and attainment of nirvana as a matter of fulfilling his own aims.

The wisdom of a buddha is something that just cannot be understood by the concepts of rational, dualistic mind, the kind of mind that ordinary beings have. Wisdom, which is the name for the particular type of mind that a buddha has, is just outside the scope of rational mind[18]. It cannot be fathomed or plumbed by a rational type of mind. Therefore, ***his wisdom is unfathomable***. Note that this does not mean that a buddha possesses an unfathomable amount of a "wise" kind of mind. It means that he has wisdom, and wisdom is something altogether beyond the scope of rational mind.

One of the many qualities of wisdom is that, when you have it, you have the ultimate kind of confidence. You have an absence of fear in the sense that you know that you can do anything and could express anything. Thus, ***his confidence is inconceivable***. As in the last quality, here again, "inconceivable" means beyond the range of ordinary, conceptual mind.

A buddha has removed all impurities from his being. Because of this, the special name "complete purity" is given to the various aspects of his being. For example, a buddha in general is said to consist of the two purities in which case it is talking about the complete purity that is

---

[18] Tib. blo. Rational mind is a specific term that sums up mind when it is functioning dualistically—investigating, comparing, and knowing in a mode that involves this and that. It is, except in special cases, a pejorative term.

his dharmakāya and the complete purity that is his form kāyas. In this case, it is referring to the complete purity of speech. This gives the sense of a buddha having gone beyond the speech of an ordinary being. The speech of an ordinary being and a buddha are two, very different processes. A buddha's speech comes via a wisdom mind that pervades all. When that mind creates speech, it comes from a wisdom mind which itself is complete purity. The resulting speech of complete purity has none of the faults that could normally be attributed to speech and has all of the unusual qualities that go with something that is produced from wisdom. For example, when a buddha speaks, it might seem to each person who is hearing it to be the ordinary speech of a clear-minded and well-spoken person. If those beings were to discuss it later, they would find that each of them heard, in their own language, what they needed to hear. There are many extraordinary qualities of a buddha's speech that come from its being complete purity. Thus it says, ***his speech is complete purity***.

Moreover, a buddha's speech has many rhythms and tones within it. Traditionally it is explained as having six root characteristics, each of which have ten specific aspects, making a total of sixty intonations altogether. For this reason it is exceptionally pleasing to hear. Therefore, ***his melody is pleasing***.

Not only is his voice very pleasing to hear but, as described earlier, his form is very pleasing to see. Everything about his body is perfect and his skin has a wonderful glow to it. No matter how much a person views it, the person cannot get enough of it, cannot take himself away from looking at it. Therefore, ***one never has enough of viewing the image of his body***. No-one else in the world has a bodily form like his, therefore, ***his body is unparalleled***.

Next comes a listing of some of the qualities of his liberation.

First, ***He is not contaminated by the things of desire. He is very much not contaminated by the things of form. He is not mixed with the things of formlessness***. These three sentences indicate that the Buddha has transcended the places of samsara. Buddhist tradition sums up the entirety of samsara into three planes of existence and enumerates many places of existence within each plane. The coarsest plane of existence, and hence the lowest and first mentioned, is the desire realm. It includes six major places of existence: the abodes of hell-beings, pretas, animals, humans, asuras, and gods of the desire-realm. A more subtle plane of existence, and hence the next one mentioned, is the form realm. It contains many abodes of god-like beings in four main strata. The most subtle plane of existence, and hence the last one mentioned, is the formless realm. It includes many abodes of beings who have a mental existence only and who live in four main strata. These beings are at the peak of samsaric existence. Each plane of existence has specific types of delusion, specific types of affliction, associated with it.

The Buddha lived, went to, and taught within the various places of the desire realm. Despite that, he was not contaminated by the things, meaning the afflictions, specific to the desire realm. Similarly, he fully experienced the various mental absorbtions that constitute all of the various places of the form realm. The various things specific to that realm are more subtle than the desire realm so he was not just not contaminated by them but was very much not contaminated by them. Finally, he did not live, teach, etcetera within the various places of the formless realms therefore the various things specific to that realm were just not mixed in with him to begin with. All in all, his wisdom mind remains unaffected by any and every type of samsaric mind so is beyond samsaric possibilities of mind altogether.

Because he has transcended all of samsaric existence, he has also passed beyond all the unsatisfactoriness associated with that type of existence. When the Buddha talked about the nature of samsaric existence, he said that it was "unsatisfactory". He used a term "duḥkha" which includes actual suffering but means much more than that. The term duḥkha is one of a pair of terms, the other is "sukha", which is usually translated as but does not mean, "bliss". The real meaning of dukḥa is "everything on the side of bad, not good, uncomfortable, unpleasant, not nice" and conversely of sukha is "everything on the side of good, comfortable, pleasant, nice". Thus, the term duḥkha means "unsatisfactory in every possible way." Thus, ***he is completely liberated from the sufferings*** actually means that he has completely liberated himself from the unsatisfactoriness of samsara, which includes all types of actual suffering and happiness, too.

"Completely liberated" is a specific term in Buddhism with a specific meaning. It would be too much to write about it here. However, the next quality mentions that he is "utterly completely liberated". It sounds perhaps odd but it is correct in Buddhist terms. It means that he has utterly attained complete liberation from the skandhas.

Then, ***he is utterly completely liberated from the skandhas. He does not possess dhātus. His āyatanas are restrained.*** When the Buddha began teaching, he did so by teaching what was needed to develop disenchantment with samsara in the minds of his followers. A large portion of his teaching involved clear descriptions of the psycho-physical makeup and the perceptual process of beings living in samsara. In this description, a samsaric being has a psycho-physical makeup that consists of a pile[19] of different components, called the skandhas. And in this description, a samsaric being has a perceptual process that consists of three main things: bases[20], igniters[21], and deluded consciousnesses that result from the first two. Thus, the first sentence here points out that the Buddha has completely and utterly gone beyond the psycho-physical make-up of a samsaric being. The next two sentences are saying that he is beyond the perceptual process of a samsaric being. Firstly, he does not have the bases required for samsaric perceptions. Secondly, even though he does have the igniters that could produce samsaric perceptions, he has restrained them so that they do not produce that kind of perception. In short, the Buddha has liberated himself from the constraints of samsaric skandhas, āyatanas, and dhātus, and his being

---

[19] Skt. skandha.

[20] Skt. dhātu.

[21] Skt. āyatana.

functions in a manner that is different from that of a being in samsara.

There are eighteen dhātus. "Dhātu" is a Sanskrit word with many meanings; here it means something that is a basis for a process and the particular process here is the process of samsaric perception. The eighteen dhātus consist of three sets of six: the objects registered by the eye, ear, nose, tongue, body, and mind sense faculties, the faculties that sense them, and the consciousnesses generated by the six faculties—these eighteen are mentioned in *The Heart Sutra* in a brief form when it says, "no eye, no ear", etcetera. Note that the sense faculties are not the gross physical organs such as the eyeball but are the subtle things within those organs that empower them, enabling them to give rise to consciousness. The Buddha made a point of teaching the dhātus because they are a listing of all the things that are bases for samsaric perceptions and hence root causes of samsaric existence. Thus, to say that the Buddha ***does not possess dhātus*** means that his buddha type of existence does not have any of the bases that would produce a samsaric type of person with samsaric types of perception.

There are twelve āyatanas or igniters. They are the objects registered by the six sense faculties and the six sense faculties themselves. In other words, they are the same things that are mentioned as the first twelve dhātus described above. However, the Buddha gathered them together as a group separately from the dhātus specifically to identify the igniters that cause samsaric consciousness to flare up. They are the igniters of samsaric consciousness and as such are a crucial part of the evolution of samsaric existence. If they were simply eliminated, you would have a kind of non-existence that would be useless to others. Therefore, the possibility is taught that, rather than just eliminating them, they could be restrained so as to produce a non-samsaric style of being. The subject of āyatanas is very profound, and was taught not only in the sutras but in the tantras as well. In the sutra approach, the āyatanas are explained as part of the problem; in the tantric approach they are explained as part of the solution. ***His āyatanas are restrained*** means that he is not like samsaric beings whose āyatanas run rampant and cause suffering now and later; his āyatanas have been drawn back and are held away from operating like that.

The next four epithets go together and indicate that the Buddha has totally abandoned the causes of unsatisfactoriness. Ju Mipham explains the four as two pairs by putting the knots together with craving and the torments together with the river. He sums up the way that these four work together in his commentary with,

> "This is saying that craving binds beings like knots and the river of the afflictions carries beings away, tormenting them; the Buddha is liberated from this set of four."

A sentient being's mind is a complex apparatus that contains causes for more of the same kind of mind to be produced. To become a buddha, this complex apparatus has to be dismantled. To dismantle it totally, the causes for its further production have to be removed. The key things that hold mind together and cause its continuation are like knots that hold it in place. When these knots that hold it together are undone, the causes of samsara are removed and the pure wisdom of a truly complete buddha can manifest. The Buddha has undone these knots completely so ***he has totally cut the knots***. Normally, "knots" is one of many words for "affliction". However, knots here does not mean affliction in general but is a specific reference to craving.

The afflictions that bind sentient beings into samsara are like torments; they continually give sentient beings a hard time both in the moment they are experienced and in the future, when their karmic result appears as more of the unsatisfactoriness of samsara. Buddha has abandoned all of them, therefore, ***he is completely liberated from the torments***.

Craving was highlighted by the Buddha as a principal cause of samsara. It is the key point in the twelve links of dependent origination that ties a being into the process of further becoming. As Lord Tsongkhapa says in his *Great Stages of the Path to Enlightenment*[22] "Craving selects, nourishes, and gives power to a particular karmic seed so that it is selected as the cause of a future birth and given the power needed to produce that birth". The Buddha has liberated himself from it, therefore, ***he is liberated from craving***.

The torments are like a river with a powerful current that carries beings along helplessly into more samsara. A

---

[22] This comes from the interdependent arising section of the *Great Stages of the Path to Enlightenment*, a translation of which is available for free download from the PKTC web-site.

buddha has eliminated all these causes and, in doing so, has safely crossed over the river. Therefore, ***he has crossed over the river***.

A buddha has not only abandoned the causes of the unsatisfactoriness of samsara but has also attained the fruition, the cessation of nirvana. The next epithets concern his attainment and what the realization that goes with it is like.

The Buddha, having left behind the dualistic mind of samsara, has returned to his original state, wisdom. For the sake of explaining a buddha's qualities to disciples, wisdom is often enumerated in many ways—two, five, oceans of, and so on—wisdoms. No matter how many wisdoms you want to attribute to a buddha, he has all of them, totally complete, with no aspect of any of them missing. This is explained by saying ***his wisdom is totally complete***.

What is a buddha? In fact, he is wisdom, so if you ask where a buddha resides, the answer is that he resides in his own wisdom. Wisdom is not a different thing for each person, it is just the most basic quality of knowing that there is. In that sense, the wisdom of the buddhas is the same thing. Therefore, ***he abides in the wisdom of the buddha bhagavats who arise in the past, present, and future***. Note that this is not saying that all buddhas have one mind or a universal consciousness; it is just saying that buddha resides in that wisdom which is the same wisdom that all of the buddha's have attained, are attaining, or will attain.

Now what is the quality of that wisdom? It is described in two ways. Firstly, ***he does not abide in nirvana*** is a way of pointing out that his wisdom is one that is truly transcendent over all stuck possibilities. Obviously, he has transcended samsara to get to his wisdom. However, there is the possibility that he is abiding in the nirvana of an arhat of the Lesser Vehicle. The arhat of the Lesser Vehicle has overcome the afflictions and so has passed beyond samsara but he is still abiding in, with attachment to, the nirvana that he has found. This is not total liberation from samsara; it is still a case of being trapped. Thus, the Buddha has not only transcended samsara but has also passed beyond the trap of abiding in the Lesser Vehicle nirvana.

Secondly, if the Buddha does not abide in either of the two extremes of samsara and nirvana, then where does he abide? The sutra says, ***he abides in the limit of the authentic itself***. This is a standard way of talking in ancient India. The word for limit is actually the same word as "extreme" just used in the last paragraph. He does not abide in the extremes of samsara or nirvana but does abide in the extreme, so to speak, of having entered ultimate reality, which is also known as "the authentic". Here you could understand "limit" as "final point". Ultimate reality is not an extreme in the sense of a place where you are stuck but is the limit, the final point, that is possible.

What does he do at that level? It says, ***he abides on the level of looking upon all sentient beings***. Firstly, a buddha does not know all phenomena in the way that ordinary beings know many things; a buddha's knowing is non-dual wisdom, not the dualistic consciousness of sentient beings. The way that wisdom operates is fundamentally different from consciousness. One of the features of wisdom is that it knows everything, all at once, and that is the quality that is being referred to here. It is precisely because a buddha is completely freed from the trap of skandhas, dhātus, and āyatanas that his buddha nature is thoroughly manifest, and, dwelling in that state of mind, he "knows" all phenomena, including all sentient beings, effortlessly and spontaneously.

Secondly, the wisdom of a truly complete buddha is focussed not on one or a few or even many sentient beings but constantly has every single sentient being as its reference. This is the bodhichitta of a buddha, a bodhichitta which does not merely have an aspiration to benefit all beings but is actually cognizant of every being in every moment and is actively engaged in doing whatever could be done for all of those beings in every given moment. Such is the power of a buddha.

The third main part of the section on buddha's qualities is the conclusion that says, ***these are the true qualities of the greatness of the body of the buddha bhagavat***. This sums up the section on the qualities of a buddha by saying that the qualities mentioned really are the qualities of a buddha. Here, "body" means the being as a whole of a buddha, it does not mean the form bodies of a buddha. You could say, "Truly, these are the good qualities of the greatness that is the being of a buddha".

B. The Qualities of Dharma

This is in two parts. The first part is a summary and the second part is a more extensive explanation.

The summary section consists of what are called "the three goodnesses", "the two excellences", and "the four conducts of purity".

The holy dharma is good in the beginning, good in the middle, and good at the end sums up the good qualities of dharma. Some years after the Buddha started teaching the dharma, the word had spread across India that these teachings were available and there was a demand for the teaching that the Buddha personally could not fulfill. By that time, there were a number of monks in his community who had a good grasp of his teaching and good realization. Therefore, he sent several of them off with the injunction to spread the word of the Buddha. At the time, he famously reminded them that the dharma was always good: "Good in the beginning, good in the middle, and good in the end". This is true generally of course: the actual dharma has no blemish or obscuration anywhere; it is reality itself or teaching that accords with that reality. Thus, it is always perfect.

The explanation given by Ju Mipham is that the first steps of dharma, the practice of it after that, and the realization that comes of it in the end all are good. He equates these steps with hearing, contemplating, and meditating. In other words, the dharma is good right from the day you first hear it all the way through until you fully realize it.

Ju Mipham also pointed out that the three could be seen as an expression of the stages of practice. The Vidyadhara took this traditional explanation and commented in his own unique way, saying that, even though the dharma is always perfect, we sometimes have a tendency to gloss over parts of it or our practice as being less meaningful, not meaningful, and so on. These words remind us that the practice of dharma is "on" all the time and that every bit of it is good and is meaningful. When you understand this point of dharma, it tends to bring a lot of brilliance into your life because your whole life is seen as non-stop goodness.

Now this dharma has two specific qualities of excellence. Firstly, the teaching of the dharma deals only with what is real and how to get to that reality. In doing so, it leaves aside all teaching on meaningless subjects or subjects that are of little real meaning and concerns itself only with the subject of removing the ignorance of sentient beings. Therefore ***its meaning is excellent***, that is to say, its meaning is only always excellent. Secondly, the wording of the teaching is always good and precise. There is no bad expression, poor composition, unnecessary wording, or any of the other usual faults of composition in it. Instead, the composition is always good. Two features of good composition are that the composition says just what needs to be said for, and in words that can be understood by, the person who receives it. This quality is very evident in the teachings of dharma given by a buddha. When you read the sutras or other words of the Buddha that have been translated into English, you will often get the sense of just how well chosen and put together are his words. That is what it means when it says, ***its wording is*** *excellent*. Here "wording" is a grammatical term that means the choice of words, phrases, and expressions used to impart the meaning.

Then, this dharma has four specific qualities known as the "Four Conducts of Purity". This name is connected with ancient Indian religious culture and its meaning is not readily obvious. In ancient India, the priests of the Hindu religion prized pure behaviour as the path to godhood. The god "Braḥmā" for them was the ultimate purity of godliness and "charyā" was behaviour or conduct, so Braḥmācharyā as it they called it was the prized norm for religious behaviour.

The term "braḥmācharyā" was so pervasive that it had to become part of the Buddhist vocabulary. It was used in Buddhism in the conventional sense of purity of behaviour of a practitioner. For example, abstaining from sex as a practice, vowed or otherwise, was called "braḥmācharya". However, it also had a special meaning and that is the meaning here. The purity of the dharma, which is the ultimate purity for Buddhists, was also called "braḥmā" meaning "a purity of someone who has attained the ultimate purity". And then, anything that accorded with that ultimate kind of purity would get the name of "braḥmācharyā" meaning something was "the way of ultimate purity". Thus these next four qualities are called "the four braḥmācharyās" in the sense of four aspects of dharma which are the ways of the ultimate purity of the dharma.

The first purity is that ***it is not adulterated***. The Buddha's dharma has parts that sound like the teachings of other religions. However, unlike the teachings of other religions, the Buddha's teaching comes from someone who has fully seen reality and who, driven only by love and compassion, strives only to bring others to that reality. Therefore, the Buddhadharma is an uncommon teaching, and does not have lesser or mistaken teachings mixed in with it. The literal wording of the sutra is that "it is not mixed up with anything" meaning that it is quite distinct from these other, more common types of teaching and does not have that lesser kind of meaning mixed in with it. It is something that accords with the ultimate purity in that it has no impurity mixed in with it.

The second purity is that it ***is totally complete***. The Buddha's dharma is like medicine for the disease of the afflictions. However, it is not a partial cure for just one affliction or another. Rather, it is a complete cure, one that deals with the entirety of afflictions that appear throughout the three realms of existence.

The third purity is that it ***is total purity***. The teachings of the dharma are shown for the purpose of bringing the complete purity that is the nature of all dharmas to the attention of sentient beings. Complete purity was mentioned before in relation to Buddha's speech and it is the same concept here. No dharma in the entirety of the dharmadhātu, the entirety of the range of all phenomena, has ever had any samsaric impurity within its nature; all dharmas are fundamentally a nature of complete purity to begin with. This quality is that the conventional dharma is talking about the pre-existing purity that is the ground state of reality.

The final purity is connected to the third one, ***is total purification***. Because the ground situation is total purity, the path of dharma can be applied to purify any given sentient being and be successful. A sentient being is said to be in "total affliction", which is like saying "total impurity". By applying the path, the impurity of the afflictions is removed. Once the work of purifying is complete, the sentient being has left behind "total affliction" and, having arrived at "total purification", has returned to his original condition. Here total purification specifically refers to the result of having become purified after doing the work of purification. In other words, another aspect of the dharma teaching is that it has the power to take one to the total purity mentioned as the last quality.

Now there is the extensive explanation of the good qualities of the dharma. This has its own summary and extensive explanation.

The summary is the sentence ***the bhagavat has taught the dharma well***. The literal meaning of the words, that the dharma is taught in a good style, is not the point here. The meaning here actually is "the dharma that the buddha bhagavat teaches is good dharma because what he teaches is true dharma properly taught". This epithet of the dharma arose in ancient India when the Buddhists of the time were making the point that the dharma taught by the Buddha was good compared to the dharma taught by other religious leaders.

The more extensive part of the extensive explanation begins here and continues to the end of the recollection of the good qualities of dharma. It shows the qualities of the dharma firstly from the perspective that it is free of faults and secondly from the perspective that it possesses good qualities.

First, there is a set of three statements starting with "It is authentic sight". These show the ways in which the dharma taught by a buddha bhagavat is well taught, that is, it is good dharma.

The Buddha himself, having unmistakenly seen the situation of phenomena has taught the meaning accordingly. Therefore, beings who rely on that dharma to tame themselves will be able, unmistakenly, to see reality. Therefore, the dharma ***is authentic sight***. The dharma is a case of correct vision in operation. The buddha has correct vision, so he teaches the dharma accordingly, and that means that sentient beings who rely on that teaching also have the ability to gain correct vision. It is a case of correct vision throughout. "The authentic", as before, is a name for reality. The buddha has sight of the authentic, and that means that sentient beings who rely on that teaching also have the ability to gain sight of the authentic. The dharma is a case of sight of the authentic, throughout.

It is free from sickness. Sickness is counted as a manifestation of affliction. This dharma that removes the afflictions and their latencies is never defiled with affliction, like a sun which itself never darkens.

Its time has no interruption. This way of talking comes from ancient India. It means that there is never any point in time when the dharma loses its effectiveness. It is like saying, "dharma could never take a break". That is so because reality is always present and never ceases and the dharma teaching is nothing other than an expression of that reality. If you were to say that this meant, "It is always timely", it would give the impression that dharma teachings have a knack of coming on time, etc. However, this is not about the magical quality of auspicious co-incidence; this is saying that dharma is always effective, that there is never a break in the continuity of its being effective.

Gampopa continually pointed out to his great yogin disciples such as the first Karmapa, Dusum Khyenpa, in his replies to their questions that one of the qualities of Mahāmudrā is that it is "on at all times". What he was talking about and what is being said here are the same. This is the way that Kagyus would discuss this[23].

Next come three statements that show not that it is free of fault but that it possesses good qualities.

It brings one in. The dharma, which represents the final blissful state in which samsara with all of its problems has been left behind, serves to take hold of the mindstream and bring it in closer and closer to that state. Finally, it brings you right into the state of final ease and bliss. The original phrase here in Sanskrit refers to a guru

---

[23] You can read Gampopa's question and answer interviews with his main disciples in a forthcoming book from PKTC that contains all of his records all of his interviews with Phagmo Drupa, Dusum Khyenpa, and two other of his chief yogin disciples.

who takes the disciple by the shoulders and draws him up very close then, when he is there, gives him the empowerment into the final state. The dharma takes you by the shoulders and guides you in, gradually bringing you in out of the various states of samsaric existence, then it also does the final work of bringing you right into the final state of emancipation.

Seeing it is meaningful. Sentient beings are stuck in the mire of existence with its unceasing torment and will remain stuck there until they meet the dharma, recognize it for what it is, and then practise it. If someone were to throw them a rope from the far side of the mire, and they were to recognize it as the way out once and for all, they could grasp the rope and use it to get truly free. Nothing else could be more meaningful for them in the mire, and likewise nothing could be more meaningful for sentient beings than to meet with the dharma thus, "seeing it is meaningful".

It is known to the wise through individual self-knowing. This dharma is extremely profound, one whose reality cannot be directly known by the ordinary, rational mind that belongs to people in the samsaric world. No matter how clever that rational mind is, it will not be able to see the actual reality that the words of the dharma point towards.

The "wise" ones here specifically refers to those who are expert in this matter of seeing reality. They are the noble ones—as fully discussed earlier—who actually see, in direct perception, the reality that the words of dharma point towards. What is it about these noble ones that makes them expert enough to be able to know the profound meaning in direct perception? It is specifically that they have something more than rational mind; they have, through their practice, uncovered the specific type of insight called "individual self-knowing" and it is through this specific insight that they can see profound reality directly.

This term "individual self-knowing" normally needs a lot of explanation but, basically, it means that kind of mind that is not looking outwards at phenomena but which is looking inside at its own nature. The dualistic, rational-type mind of ordinary sentient beings only looks out at phenomena which seem to be over there away from itself which is here. Individual self-knowing specifically does not look outwards like that but "self-knows", that is, knows itself. In doing so, it sees all phenomena individually just exactly as they are but without dualising and making them into something concretely separate. This individual self-knowing is wisdom. Specifically, it is the aspect of wisdom that a practitioner uses on the path to see emptiness directly and so exit from samsara.

In short, the point is that the profound dharma is not known by the mind of ordinary sentient beings but is known only by those who have become somewhat expert in wisdom, sufficiently expert that they can see this meaning using the individual self-knowing aspect of wisdom.

The next quality explained is that the dharma is that which, when understood, brings certainty that it is the place to put one's trust. Again, there is a summary then a more extensive explanation.

The dharma taught by the bhagavat is properly revealed in the Vinaya is a summary. There are different phrasings of this good quality in Tibetan literature, each leading to a different translation and some to a different understanding of the meaning involved. The English here follows the wording of the text used for the translation. For an extensive explanation of this quality and the various ways of understanding it, see the companion book *Unending Auspiciousness* by the author.

After the Buddha had passed away, his followers committed all the teachings they had heard to writing. The teachings were arranged into three baskets. The first basket consisted of all the teachings concerned with the disciplines of personal liberation, which includes all of the rules and regulations for living monastic life. This section was named "Vinaya", meaning "Taming", because the teachings on discipline have the effect of taming body, speech, and mind. This quality states that the complete teaching of the Buddha is found in the teachings of the Vinaya.

When the *Sutra* was put together, monasticism was the main way to follow the Buddha's teaching. This statement confirms that the monastic way is complete and perfect as the way to follow the Buddha's dharma. In later times and other places, such as Tibet and now in the West, a different sense goes with it. Some people feel that the profound depths of dharma, such as the teachings of emptiness of the Great Vehicle, are not revealed in the Vinaya, therefore it could not contain the deep meaning of dharma. That is not the case; all teachings of the Lesser Vehicle, including the Vinaya, were taught by the Buddha himself from the space of ultimate reality that he was part of. So, there is the point for anyone following what are usually thought of as higher practices than monasticism that the Vinaya teachings do contain the full meaning of ultimate dharma and are good for taming.

Now, that summary is explained in detail with six specific qualities as follows.

The first two qualities are connected. What does the dharma presented in the Vinaya consist of, essentially speaking? ***It is renunciation***. And what does that do? ***It causes one to arrive at complete enlightenment***. "Renunciation" translates a Sanskrit word that means that you have turned towards and committed yourself to a process that is good and reliable. In other words, it refers to the positive step that you take after you are first revolted by and then renounce samsara. You do have to become revolted by samsara first; as it says in the *Short Vajradhara Prayer* of the Karma Kagyu, "Revulsion is the foot of meditation as is taught". That revulsion leads to renunciation, which is turning away from something. However, there is still a third step, which is that you now step off towards something that is good and which is worthwhile. Unfortunately, we do not have a good word for this third step in English so we always end up using the second word in the three-step process to refer to the third step. The tone of the Buddha's explanations was never the slightly negative connotation of "renunciation" but the much more positive sense of "stepping out now towards that which really is worthwhile". Doing so, as it says, causes you to arrive at the truly complete enlightenment of a buddha. Thus, even though the Vinaya seems to be a lesser teaching, it actually does function to bring you to full enlightenment and the way it does that is through renunciation which is the key point of the Vinaya teaching.

This kind of dharma taught in the Vinaya, whose essential quality is renunciation and abandonment, is not contradictory to the path of enlightenment as expressed in other places such as in the higher teachings of the Great Vehicle. The teachings as a whole were taught for sentient beings of varying capacities and inclinations and, though some might show the meaning of profound reality more explicitly than others, each teaching is still a teaching that comes from a buddha and which therefore is in accord with reality. In short, the teachings of the Vinaya are the Buddha's dharma and are not in contradiction to other teachings of that dharma. In this sense, all of the teachings of dharma, high and low, are in harmony with each other, that is, there is no inconsistency in them, therefore, ***it is without disharmony... And,*** not only are all of the teachings consistent but each one contains the meaning of each other because all of them are teachings that come from reality. And not only does each one contain the meaning of each other but all of them can be summed up into just one, all-inclusive point of reality. Therefore, the dharma teaching as a whole is not only without disharmony but also ***...does have inclusion***. In other words, each dharma teaching does contain the seeds of all the others, even if some of them appear to be contradictory on the surface.

The last property makes the dharma as a whole a place of ultimate trustworthiness. The last two properties together mean that the teaching of the Buddha as expressed in the Vinaya is a true expression of dharma and not only because it is true in its own right but because it does actually embody the entirety of the dharma teaching.

When you become the president of the United States, you achieve a position of great power and you might think that you will depend on that position to accomplish many things. However, the position itself is not truly reliable. Firstly, it will have to come to an end after some years but could end due to unexpected conditions of civil war, etcetera. Secondly, although you might intend your presidency as a platform for accomplishing certain goals, it might, due to shifts in politics or law, change in direction such that it could no longer be a platform for accomplishing those things. The dharma is not like that. Firstly, as long as you yourself do not let it go, it will always be a reliance, without any loss of capability or sudden change in capability to do so. Then, it does not change course after you have started to rely on it and veer off into being a different kind of reliance, so it is always suitable for the purpose that it was originally relied upon; once you take it up as a reliance, you can depend on it to be constantly supportive and always on course. Therefore, the dharma itself is something that is, in general, thoroughly ***reliable***. More than that though, this is the dharma that was spoken by the Buddha after he himself attained full comprehension of the totality of reality, therefore it is not just reliable but, because of being the Buddha's dharma with all that implies, ***it has*** that special kind of ***reliability***.

Moreover, some people might accept that the dharma is thoroughly reliable but might then think that it will not be a final solution. They might think that it could be relied on but that there would never be an end to having to do that. However, that is not so. Dharma practice itself is directed towards a final goal and travelling the dharma path is like taking a journey towards that goal. Once the goal has been reached, it has been reached and there is no more travelling to be done. Buddhahood is called "no more training" or "no more learning" because it is final and there is no more to be done. It is also called "having laid down the burden" which makes the point that once buddhahood has been attained, the burden of the activities of the path that was originally taken up is done with and put aside once and for all. At that point, it is not as though there is still some other thing to be done or more of the same still left to go. Therefore, ***it does end the journey***.

C. The Qualities of Sangha

The recollection of the sangha starts out with, ***as for the sangha of the great vehicle....*** The sangha here refers, as explained earlier, specifically to the noble sangha. It does not refer merely to the groups of ordinary practitioners who get the name "sangha" but who are not the refuge Jewel sangha. "Sangha of the great vehicle" here could refer to the sangha of the Great Vehicle as opposed to the Lesser Vehicle but it really refers more generally to the entirety of the noble sangha. Collectively, they are the ones who are the sangha of that great vehicle, meaning the vehicle of the buddhas in general. Another way to explain "great vehicle" is that the noble ones collectively are at the point where their specific intentions in terms of continuing on to nirvana and so forth are great, meaning beyond those of ordinary beings. These beings, having had direct sight of reality, are so convinced of their path that they are described as the ones whose "intentions never falter". These noble beings, unlike the ordinary sangha, have arrived on the great vehicle, the one in which the beings on it all have unswerving and great intentions for nirvana.

There are two parts to the recollection of this noble sangha's qualities. The first part shows them as ones who have special qualities because of having greatly purified their mindstreams. The second part praises them as a field of these highly developed good qualities which can then be a source of benefit for others, just like a good field that in turn gives rise to good harvests.

What qualities have they developed? There are four of them. Again, note that this is not a statement about qualities that will be developed by the ordinary practitioner as he goes along. Rather, this is a statement of the qualities that have been developed by the noble ones, the ones who are the sangha Jewel. Firstly, ***they have entered into good*** meaning that they have, through the principal training in discipline[24], already restrained their minds. Secondly, ***they have entered into insight*** meaning that they have already developed, through the principal training in concentration, one-pointed concentration of mind on the

---

[24] All Buddhist practice can be summed up into the three higher trainings of śhīla, samādhi, and prajñā, that is, of discipline, concentration, and discerning mind. These three are being used as the basis for the current explanation.

meaning of reality. Thirdly, ***they have entered into straightness*** meaning that they have, through the principal training in prajñā[25], already liberated themselves through having developed the prajñā of the authentic view. Fourthly, ***they have entered into harmony*** meaning that they have already entered nirvana without any discordance between the various aspects of the trainings just mentioned—view, discipline, aims of migrators, and so on.

These noble beings filled with these excellent qualities have become a field of excellence for others. Because of that, they are worthy of veneration in general. Veneration in general was done in ancient India and has been done since then in all Buddhist traditions by joining the two palms at the heart. Therefore, ***they are worthy of joined palms*** meaning that they are worthy of veneration in general. However, they are also worthy of a much higher level of respect than that, because they are a true refuge, they are the sangha Jewel. The highest level of veneration in ancient India and in all Buddhist traditions since then has been to actually prostrate to a person. Thus, because of being a true refuge, ***they are*** additionally ***worthy of prostration***.

They are a field of the glory of merit. "Field" means a basis for something to come forth. "Glory" is an ancient Indian word that means "excellence" or "perfect collection". All together, these excellent qualities that they

---

[25] The text here has related the first three to the three trainings of śhīla, samādhi, and prajñā.

have developed have made them into a field from which other sentient beings can harvest a wealth of merit.

Because the beings of the noble sangha are freed of faults and have an abundance of good qualities, even whole universes could be offered to them and they would not fall into affliction over it. They have, through their training, been fully trained in the receipt of gifts, not merely in the usual sense of learning to be nice about receiving a gift but also in the deeper sense of keeping a mind that is unaffected by any negative state in regard to the gift, and also in the deepest sense of maintaining the view of no self while receiving the gift. They have been so well trained in those ways that they are thoroughly capable of receiving any kind of gift, thus ***they are great ones thoroughly trained in gifts.***

Finally, there are two statements that continue on directly from the last and which show that these beings of excellent qualities are supreme places for making gifts and offerings. The first says that ***they are a place of generosity***. Because of the qualities that they have developed they are, as mentioned above, an excellent field from which all sorts of excellent harvests can come. Thus, in terms of giving gifts and making offerings, great benefits will arise from making offerings to them. In other words, they are the right kind of person to be generous with because generosity made in relation to them opens many doors as well as accumulating great merit, therefore, they are indeed a place of generosity. And more than that, ***they are*** in fact ***in all places even a great place for generosity*** because in all places throughout all of the worlds there is no other place of generosity comparable to them.

All in all, the mindstreams of worldly people are spoiled by afflictions but these beings are completely liberated in comparison, therefore, they are like a pure gem.

Why was the sangha picked out as a place of generosity instead of mentioning any of the many other qualities that it has? It is because this was a very great theme in earlier times. This quote from a sutra will help you to understand this point,

> "Those humans who are scared with fear
> Mostly take refuge in mountains, forests,
> Parks, and in large trees used as a place of
> offerings;
> Such refuges are not the principal one and
> Such refuges are not supreme.
> Someone who relies on such refuge
> Will not be liberated from all suffering.
> Rather, when someone has gone to the buddha,
> The dharma, and the sangha for refuge, he will,
> through
> Suffering, the source of suffering,
> True transcendence of suffering, and
> The pleasant eight-fold path of the noble ones
> Go to nirvana. With that,
> The four truths of the noble ones
> With prajñā used to produce the view
> Is his principal refuge;
> By relying on that refuge he will indeed
> Be liberated from all suffering."

It was and still is a part of many non-Buddhist traditions in India and Nepal to make daily worship of deities at the base of large, spreading trees such as the Bodhi trees that were and are common in these lands. The trees were regarded as the home of the deities by the local people and they were supplicated each morning with offerings of various sorts in order to secure protection. The Buddha made a major point about this, as for example in the sutra just quoted, in which he clearly stated that this was the wrong way to go about making offerings and seeking protection. He stated that the community of spiritually advanced Buddhist practitioners—the noble ones—are the best place for making offerings in general because of their great qualities in relation to gifts and, more than that, in the specific sense of worshipping a refuge. They are the ones worthy of offerings, they are the ones capable of properly receiving all gifts, not the deities that the common folk of India habitually went to with their offerings at the base of large trees. It is that way not because Buddha said so but because of the qualities of the mind of a person who has become a noble one on the Buddhist path and is therefore a member of the sangha Jewel.

vi. The Colophon

A sutra translated into Tibetan should always have a colophon to indicate the translator and final editor, at least. The Tibetan edition of the liturgy used for this translation does not show the ending colophon. At least one other edition of the liturgy does have it, and editions of just the sutra printed by itself also have it. Even if it were included, it would not be recited.

At this point, the chanting of the sutra is complete and with it the opening of the Oryoki set should have been completed.

2. Accepting the Food

This section is recited continuously while the food is being distributed. The food is accepted according to the Japanese form of Oryoki. This section has two parts to it.

i. Receiving Food from the Donors

Originally, a wandering mendicant received alms in a bowl or, in monastic situations, the food was received by the monastery as a donation and then distributed. The Vidyadhara encouraged a community in which each person was financially responsible for himself and paid his own way but still, with the remembrance that one is receiving food due to the efforts of others, the proper attitude can be taken up.

During the receipt of food, several verses of homage to the noble Three Jewels are chanted continuously. These are standard verses that have been in Buddhist tradition since ancient times:

The protector who possesses great kindness,
The omniscient teacher,
The basis of oceans of merit and virtue,
I prostrate to the tathāgata.

Pure, the cause of freedom from passion,
Virtuous, liberating from the lower realms,
This alone is the supreme, ultimate truth:
I prostrate to the dharma, which is peace.

Having been liberated, they show the path to liberation;
They are fully dedicated to the disciplines;
They are a holy field of merit and possess virtue:
I prostrate to the sangha.

The first verse mentions the qualities of Buddha, then pays homage to him, and then the second and third verses do the same for the dharma and sangha. In each case, the qualities mentioned are traditional ways of understanding the function of each of the noble Three Jewels as a refuge. The meaning should be plain without further explanation. These verses are all composed from words used by the Buddha himself.

The fourth verse mentions the Three Jewels and again venerates their respective functions as objects of refuge, this time in a more condensed way:

I prostrate to the Buddha, the leader;
I prostrate to the dharma, the protector;
I prostrate to the sangha, the community:
I prostrate respectfully and always to these three.

This verse is used in some Buddhist communities as a general "meal chant"done before meals. The Buddha is the leader because he shows the way to liberation, the dharma shown by him has the ability to protect from the sufferings of samsara, and the sangha is the community of noble practitioners who help others along the path. Note the use of the words "noble practitioners". Again, it is always the case that the objects of refuge, the Three Jewels, are enlightened principles. As mentioned before, "noble" is not just a nice address but has the very specific meaning of "being superior because of having transcended samsara". Here, "the sangha" refers specifically to the noble sangha, which means those who are out of samsara. It does mean the community who are the actual refuge object, and who have attained to the path of insight, which is all of the arhats of the Lesser Vehicle and the bodhisatvas who are dwelling on the bhūmis.

The last verse described the conventional qualities of each of the three objects of refuge. Because we are considering the *noble* Three Jewels, who by definition are the ones beyond samsara, their actual qualities are outside the scope of conceptual mind. When the next verse says "inconceivable" it has that meaning and does not mean simply that their qualities are enormous. The verse begins by reminding us that the virtues, here meaning good qualities, are inconceivable. Then it uses the energy of the faith aroused to create a cause which likewise is beyond normal concept, rebirth in one of the buddha fields, and ultimately buddhahood:

> *The Buddha's virtues are inconceivable;*
> *The dharma's virtues are inconceivable;*
> *The sangha's virtues are inconceivable;*
> *Having faith in these inconceivables,*
> *Therefore, the fruitions are inconceivable:*
> *May I be born in a completely pure realm.*

Rebirth in a buddha field is desirable from a practitioner's point of view because the whole environment of such a place is conducive to quick and easy completion of the path. In the traditions both of Mahāmudrā and Great Completion[26], it is said that, if you cannot manage enlightenment either in this life or in the earlier stages of the intermediate state following this life, you should at least try to go from the ending stage of the intermediate state directly to a pure field because there you can easily and definitely attain enlightenment.

It is quite surprising how much energy and how much clarity of mind can be developed by considering the qualities of the Three Jewels like this and then, on the basis of the faith aroused, paying homage to them. This way of recollecting the Three Jewels in order to bring on faith, refuge, and with them, good qualities and auspiciousness of life in general, was one of the Buddha's important instructions to his followers of the time. This shows the skill with which this text has been put together.

That is the end of receiving the food.

ii. Declaration that the Food is Proper

Next, we remind ourselves that the food has been obtained by the proper means and therefore will benefit our health. We hold up the begging bowl of food and, with this verse, declare that the food we are about to eat is in accord with the dharma:

> *Substances that have been offered to the Three Jewels and plunder from others—*

[26] Tib. rdzogs chen.

I have completely abandoned all such impure and perverted nourishment;
This food is in accord with the dharma, free from evil deeds:
May the health of my body flourish.

The teaching of the eight-fold path of the noble ones, which sums up the Lesser Vehicle path, says that food, and so on should be obtained through right livelihood and not wrong livelihood. Food obtained through wrong livelihood would be food obtained by some means that causes harm to others or that drags one further into samsara, such as killing, stealing, and so on. Since anything that has been offered to the Three Jewels is considered to belong to them, to take it and use it would be the same as using stolen goods. In older cultures where the monastic sangha was well established, it was well known amongst both the lay and monastic communities that anything given to the formal sangha—whether given to a single monk or a whole monastery—was now the property of the sangha and that stealing that or even using it for one's own purposes was a serious crime. The words here are especially referring to that idea. ***Plunder from others*** means all other cases of stolen food or food obtained in connection with theft.

Food obtained through such means is impure nourishment because of its involvement with bad karmic consequences. Eating such food actually does affect one's health adversely. On the other hand, food which has been obtained through non-involvement in negativity, and which is thus ***in accord with the dharma, free from evil deeds,*** promotes well-being both physically and mentally. A Buddhist practitioner will always take care to prepare food which is in accord with dharma. Thus, the food is presented at this point with the aspiration, ***may the health of my body flourish***.

3. Blessing, Offering, Eating the Food, and Offering the Leftovers

i. Blessing and Offering the Food

The food is offered to various beings, higher and lower, before eating oneself. The offerings as a whole are done in a Vajra Vehicle way, therefore the food is blessed into vajra food or ***divine food*** as it is also called in the text in preparation for offering and eating it. The liturgy says:

Then bless the food with:

OṂ ĀḤ HŪṂ

The mantra OṂ ĀḤ HŪṂ is said three times. The mantra consists of the seed syllables of enlightened body, speech, and mind in that order. While saying this, you should transform your perception from ordinary samsaric perception to pure perception or sacred outlook as the Vidyadhara called it. If you have not entered the Vajra Vehicle formally and received the necessary instruction, you will not know how to do this, in which case just recite the mantra and keep your mind focussed on the goodness of the situation.

The liturgy now offers two suggestions on how to divide the food up and offer it, which includes eating it.

From the "Lamp on Summed up Conduct":

> *Divide the food into four parts.*
> *First, offer pure food to the devas.*
> *After that, to the dharmapālas and protectors*
> *Offer elaborate torma.*
> *Then, eat and drink.*
> *Give the leftover, to all the bhūtas.*

In that way, or else, as is said in the Vinaya of the holy dharma, divide the food into three parts.

The Indian text *Lamp on Summed up Conduct*, a text written by the Indian master Aryadeva, says that the food should be divided into four parts.

The first part will be offered to the higher beings. The word "devas" in the text here does not mean "gods" as in samsaric gods but the higher beings who have passed beyond samsara—the gurus, buddhas, bodhisatvas, and so on.

The second part will be offered to the dharmapālas and other protectors of the dharma, which includes both enlightened and un-enlightened beings.

The third part will be an offering of several tormas to the lower beings. "Torma" is the Tibetan word for a ritual item that is supposed to be made from some kind of dough. Tibetans used to make them from roasted barley flour but any kind of cooked or uncooked doughy substance can be used. Tormas can be decorated elaborately and very beautifully but this is not required; they can be as simple as a pinch of food or other suitable offering. In Oryoki, it is single pinch of food.

The fourth portion will be food and drink taken for oneself, the leftovers of which are given to the bhūtas. Bhūta literally means "elemental" and is just the same as that word when used in English to mean all kinds of spirits. It refers to beings of the preta realm. In Oryoki, this is a small amount of food left over in one's bowl which is put into a container carried around by a server.

That is one way of approaching the food, but there is another way according to the Vinaya in which the food is divided into three portions. This method is not used in Oryoki practice.

Tibetans follow the first method in which the food is divided into four parts and then offered and eaten. The extensive set of offerings that appears at this point in the liturgy corresponds to that approach. When Tibetans say each of the offering mantras in the liturgy, they take a little bit of moistened tsampa from their bowl, make a small torma by rolling the tsampa into shape between their fingers, and place the torma on a little plate next to them. At the end, they have a set of tormas on the plate. The plate with tormas is offered and the tormas are collected at the appropriate time. The Vidyadhara did not feel that method to be suited to the form of Oryoki, so he modified it. All the offerings are made according to the liturgy but the Japanese form of representing all of them with just two torma offerings—one for the higher beings and one for the lower beings—is followed. At the first mantra, the one for offering food to the gurus, a small piece of food is taken from the first bowl with food and placed to the upper right of the table (or the base cloth if there is no table). This covers the first five offerings that will made, concluding with the dharmapālas' offering. Then, at the mantra *OṂ HĀRĪTE SVĀHĀ*, another pinch of food is taken from the first bowl and placed at the lower right, opposite the first offering. This covers the offerings for the lower beings made with the mantras down to and including ***OṂ AGRA-PIṆḌA-ĀŚIBHYAḤ SVĀHĀ***.

The offerings to the higher beings are done with this part of the liturgy:

First, offer divine food to the gurus with:

OṂ GURU-VAJRA-NAIVEDYĀ ĀḤ HŪṂ

Likewise, offer to the host of buddha, and bodhisatvas with:

OM SARVA-BUDDHA-BODHISATVEBHYO VAJRA-NAIVEDYĀ ĀḤ HŪṂ

Offer to the divine assembly of the maṇḍala of yidams with:

OṂ KĀMA-DEVA-MAṆḌALA-NAIVEDYĀ ĀḤ HŪṂ

Offer to Mañjuśhrī and others—whatever devatā you desire—for example:

OṂ MAÑJUŚHRĪ VAJRA-NAIVEDYĀ ĀḤ HŪṂ

Offer to the dharmapālas with:

OṂ ŚHRĪ DHARMAPĀLA VAJRA-NAIVEDYĀ ĀḤ HŪṂ

These offerings are done according to the Vajra Vehicle system. In the Vajra Vehicle, the Three Jewels of general Buddhism take on a special form that is specific to the Vajra Vehicle. They are not called the Three Jewels but "the three Roots": guru, yidam, and dharmapāla. The offerings made here to the higher beings are offerings to the Three Roots and are done in the order that corresponds to the natural hierarchy involved.

The highest principle of the Three Roots is the guru because he is the source of everything; as Guardian Nagārjuna pointed out, "Without the guru there isn't even the word "buddha"". The guru shows the dharma to the students and manifests as the dharma protectors, so those two principles come after the guru. Therefore, you ***first offer the divine food to the gurus*** by saying *OṂ GURU VAJRA NAIVEDYĀ ĀḤ HŪṂ*. "Naivedyā" means "food", and "vajra-naivedyā" means "vajra food", so the mantra means, "The vajra food for the gurus". The OṂ, ĀḤ, and HŪṂ syllables bracketing the mantra are the seed syllables of enlightened body, speech, and mind and when you have the necessary teaching on that, you can bring enlightened being down on the spot as you say the mantra.

The buddhas and bodhisatvas could not be left out and they are the next highest principle so it says, ***likewise, offer to the host of buddhas and bodhisatvas with OṂ SARVA-BUDDHA-BODHISATTVEBHYO VAJRA-NAIVEDYĀ ĀḤ HŪṂ***. This mantra means "The vajra food for all the buddhas and bodhisatvas" and the OṂ, ĀḤ, and HŪṂ bracketing the mantra have the same meaning as before.

In the Vajra Vehicle, the guru shows the dharma to the disciples in the form of the second of the Three Roots, the yidam deity. Thus, ***offer to the divine assembly of the maṇḍala of yidams with OṂ KĀMA-DEVA-MAṆḌALA-NAIVEDYĀ ĀḤ HŪṂ***. The mantra means, "The food for the maṇḍala of kāma-devas". "Maṇḍala" here means "the complete world of" and "kāma-deva" means the deity, that is, yidam, of one's choice. That in turn is explained in the Vajra Vehicle in connection with the throwing of the flower during empowerment. Note that the VAJRA was left out of VAJRA-NAIVEDYĀ in the original Tibetan text, but the meaning is still the same—we are offering vajra food. The OṂ, ĀḤ, and HŪṂ bracketing the mantra have the same meaning as before.

There are various levels of deity in the tantras. The yidams to whom we have just made an offering are the deities of the highest level of the four tantras. Next we offer to the various deities of the lesser tantras such as Mañjuśhrī, Tārā, Avalokiteśhvara, and so on with ***offer to Mañjuśhrī and the others—whatever devatā you desire—for example, OṂ MAÑJUŚHRĪ VAJRA-NAIVEDYĀ ĀḤ HŪṂ.*** Here "devatā" means "deity". The mantra given means "The vajra food for Mañjuśhrī", though, as it says, you could insert, instead of "Mañjuśhrī", the name of any deities that you prefer. For simplicity's sake "Mañjuśhrī" is used by Tibetans and that is what is done in the Oryoki practice as well. The OṂ, ĀḤ, and HŪṂ bracketing the mantra have the same meaning as before.

In the Vajra Vehicle, the guru manifests as protective principles for the disciple, called the dharmapālas meaning "dharma protectors". They are the third of the Three Roots and we offer to them next with ***offer to the dharmapālas with OṂ ŚHRĪ DHARMAPĀLA VAJRA-NAIVEDYĀ ĀḤ HŪṂ.*** "Śhrī" means "glorious" thus this mantra means, "The vajra food for the glorious dharma protectors". The OṂ, ĀḤ, and HŪṂ bracketing the mantra have the same meaning as before.

At this point, the offerings to the higher beings have been completed. Next offerings are made to lower beings. There are, in terms of offerings, two types of lower beings. Some lower beings have sufficiently good karma that they can receive better quality food. Some have such bad karma that they can only receive leftovers. The offerings being made here are for beings who can get to and use a better quality of food. The liturgy says,

Offer divine food to all the bhūtas with:

OṂ A-KĀRO MUKHAṂ SARVA-DHARMĀṆĀṂ
ĀDYANUTPANNATVĀT OṂ ĀḤ HŪṂ PHAṬ SVĀHĀ

Give one pinch of food to Hārītī with:

OṂ HĀRĪTE SVĀHĀ

and one pinch of food to the five hundred sons of Hārītī with:

OṂ HĀRĪTE MAHĀYAKṢHIṆĪ HARA HARA SARVA-RĀYAṆI-KṢHIṂ SVĀHĀ

Give one pinch of food to the bhūtas who are capable of receiving the select portion with:

OṂ AGRA-PIṆḌA-ĀŚHIBHYAḤ SVĀHĀ

The first offering is made with ***offer divine food to all the bhūtas with OṂ A-KĀRO MUKHAṂ SARVA-DHARMĀṆĀM ĀDYANUTPANNATVĀT OṂ ĀḤ HŪṂ PHAṬ SVĀHĀ***. The mantra means, "The syllable A is foremost because of the unoriginatedness of all dharmas". The ĀḤ in OṂ ĀḤ HŪṂ is the seed syllable of enlightened speech; the A here is more primordial even; it is the seed syllable of primordial un-originatedness. Kāro means "syllable"; mukhaṃ usually means "face" but in this case it means "foremost"; sarva means "all"; and dharmāṇām is the genitive plural meaning "of dharmas". In ādyanutpannatvāt, the tvāt means "ness", anutpana means "non-arising", and ādya means "etcetera"; all together it means "the non-originatedness" or "the unborn-ness".

This mantra is always done preliminary to the actual offerings for lower beings because it prepares the offering for them in a special way. Through it, when the pretas partake of the offering, their perception is transformed, at least momentarily, into sacred outlook, or pure perception. Thus the offering substance becomes more than just sustenance for them, and the offering becomes a special offering of the dharma. From that point of view, its repetition is a direct expression of çompassion for these unfortunate beings.

Having prepared the offering for the pretas as a whole with the OṂ A-KĀRO mantra, an offering is first made to Hārītī and her five hundred sons. Hārītī was a great yakṣhiṇī who lived at the time of the Buddha. Yakṣhas and yakṣhiṇīs—male and female respectively—are beings of the preta realm. They are semi-human in appearance, bloodthirsty, and nasty; they are the same things as the trolls and hobgoblins of European cultures, and are sometimes very powerful. There are representations of Hārītī in Indian sculptings that show her story. Now, Hārītī had a family of five hundred sons and the only way that she could feed them all was to kill animals. The Buddha heard of this and decided to put an end to it so he kidnapped her youngest son, whose name was Piṇḍala, and hid him under his begging bowl. Since Piṇḍala was the youngest son, he was also Hārītī's dearest, so she searched for him everywhere. Someone suggested to her that the Buddha might know of Piṇḍala's whereabouts because of his great powers, so Hārītī went to the Buddha and asked for help in finding her son Piṇḍala. The Buddha said that he knew of Piṇḍala's whereabouts but that he really disapproved of the killing that Hārītī was doing and would not say where Piṇḍala was unless she would promise to stop the slaughter. Hārītī complained that she would not be able to feed her family if she stopped killing so the Buddha said that he would have his sangha put aside some food from each meal for her and her sons. She said that that would be good but what about when the Buddha was gone? He assured her that his sangha would always take care of her and her sons and she agreed to stop killing. Thus, in the Buddhist tradition, the offerings to lower beings usually start with an offering especially for Hārītī and her five hundred sons. So here ***we give one pinch of food to Hārītī with*** **OṂ HĀRĪTE SVĀHĀ**, ***and one pinch to the five hundred sons of Hārītī with*** **OṂ HĀRĪTE MAHĀYAKṢHIṆĪ HARA HARA SARVA RĀYAṆIKṢHIṂ SVĀHĀ**.

Next, we ***give a pinch of food to the bhūtas who are capable of receiving the select portion***. Pretas in general have a very miserable rebirth. It is hallmarked by their inability to obtain food or drink and the extreme suffering caused by that. Some of them are slightly better off than others because they can sometimes obtain food which has been offered properly and specifically for them. Thus, as a matter of compassionate concern, whenever we partake of food ourselves, we always remember the pretas and offer them some food. For pretas in general, the food offered must be of poorer quality, otherwise their karmic situation will not let them even perceive the food. Thus we give them leftovers after the meal rather than some of the better quality offering before the meal. However, there are a few pretas who, because of having performed some good act of generosity in a prior birth, are able to obtain and consume food which is better than leftover. In order to relieve them from their extreme torment of hunger and thirst, we offer them some of the first food of the meal, a portion taken before we start eating. This portion is called the ***select portion*** and it is blessed with the mantra ***OṂ AGRA-PIṆḌA-ĀŚIBHYAḤ SVĀHĀ*** which means, "For the blessing of the select portion". "Agra" means "finest", or "best", "piṇḍa" means "a little bit of food, a morsel", and "āśhibhyaḥ" means "for the blessing of".

ii. Eating the Food

The offerings prior to eating are complete but before eating, any poison or injurious substances which might have been placed in the food are purified. The liturgy says,

If one wishes to purify any poison or the like in the food, chant:

> NAMAḤ SARVA-BUDDHA-BODHISATVĀNĀṂ OṂ BALIṂ TE JVĀLA-BALIṂ NI SVĀHĀ

Repeat this eight times; pick up food with the thumb and ring fingers, and eat.

To purify the food, the mantra, ***NAMAḤ SARVA-BUDDHA-BODHISATTVĀNĀṂ OṂ BALIṂ TE JVĀLA-BALIṂ NI SVĀHĀ*** is recited while holding up the food to be purified.

"Namaḥ" means "homage", "sarva-buddha-bodhisattvānāṃ" means "to all the buddhas and bodhisatvas", "baliṃ" is the Sanskrit word for the Tibetan word "torma" which means here food offering, and jvāla means "blazing". So all together it means, "Homage to all the buddhas and bodhisatvas, here is a torma for you, the blazing torma". In Oryoki, the first bowl that is filled with food, whichever it is, is held up during the repetition of the mantra.

The mantra does have a story behind it. There was a Braḥmin man who despised the Buddha and wanted to kill him. The Braḥmin invited the Buddha and his followers to a meal and offered them poisoned food. Because of his great powers, the Buddha knew what the patron was trying to do, so he had one of his followers chant this mantra over the food before it was served. The mantra rendered harmless the poison in the food so neither the Buddha nor any of his followers was harmed. When the Braḥmin saw the Buddha's power, he confessed and took refuge in the Three Jewels.

The instruction to eat by picking up the food with thumb and ring fingers is not followed, rather, the Japanese form of eating from the bowls with chopsticks and spoon is used. Food generally presents us with a situation rich in possibilities for samsaric involvement and usually arouses all sorts of afflictions. Oryoki gives a form to eating that can be used as an anchor for maintaining the shamatha-vipashyana practice that will counter those possibilities of samsaric involvement. For the beginner, the Lesser Vehicle discipline of shamatha-vipashyana, particularly in relation to the form of Oryoki, will be important. There will be a greater emphasis on the afflictions as something to be avoided and one might well emphasize seeing the food as impure. As one's practice matures, the style of renunciation evolves so that the afflictions are seen as poisons which are unnecessary but useful. Unnecessary because they cloud the buddha nature; useful because they become the means of continually wakening one's bodhichitta. That is the development of Oryoki practice into a Great Vehicle practice. There are still further possibilities of it becoming Vajra Vehicle practice. For example, one could approach the whole practice as feast practice and, going even further, the senses could turn into an un-interrupted flow of un-outflowed bliss during the whole meal session.

At this point the liturgy gives some advice on eating:

While eating, eat with an attitude that sees the food as impure, with an attitude of non-attachment, with an attitude that benefits the masses of different intestinal bacteria, and with an attitude of remaining on the ship that travels to peace and enlightenment. Do not eat with an attitude that increases passion and craving. In "Entrance to the Bodhisatva's Conduct" it is said, "One should eat moderately." The way of doing this is explained according to the "Ashtanga": "Two quarters of the stomach are for food; one quarter is for drink, and one quarter is left empty." Or else, according to the text "Handbook of Food": "One should have two-thirds for food and drink, and leave one-third empty."

You are encouraged to follow that advice. Of course, it is up to each person to judge how much food is needed for the health of the body; the main point here is to approach food as a way of increasing health, rather than the usual manner which drags us further into samsara which in itself is an unhealthy state. So, being mindful of the forms of Oryoki, such as neither overloading your bowl nor refusing what is offered, take what you need and enjoy your meal!

iii. Offering the Leftovers

After the food has been eaten, the liturgy says,

Finally, give a pinch of food to the bhūtas who are capable of receiving the leftovers with:

OṂ UCCHIṢHṬA-PIṆḌA-ĀŚHIBHYAḤ SVĀHĀ

As explained earlier, most pretas cannot receive or use the offering of the select portion but many can obtain sustenance from leftovers. These beings are even less fortunate than the pretas who can receive the select portion so it is important to offer food to them. To offer the leftovers to these beings the mantra ***OṂ UCCHIṢṬA-PIṆḌA-ĀŚHIBHYAḤ SVĀHĀ*** is said over the leftover food. It means "For the blessing of the leftover morsels". "Ucchiṣṭa" means "leftover"; "piṇḍa" and "āśhibhyaḥ" are the same as in the offering mantra for the select portion.

That is the end of blessing, offering, eating the food, and offering the leftovers.

4. Repaying the Kindness of the Donors

This begins the closing phase of the meal. ***Then,*** the liturgy says, the first thing to do is to ***wash the mouth.*** Provision is made for this step in the form of Oryoki. Once that is done, the Oryoki set is closed.

It is traditional that, when alms are received for the sustenance of your practice, something must be done in return for the donor. That is done now, as the Oryoki set is being closed.

Then, the liturgy says to ***purify the gift,*** which is done by saying the next section:

> *I prostrate to the bhagavat, tathāgata, arhat, saṃyaksaṃbuddha Samantaprabharaja:*
>
> NAMAḤ SAMANTAPRABHĀRĀJĀYA TATHĀGATĀYA ARHATE SAṂYAKSAṂBUDDHĀYA / NAMO MAÑJUŚHRĪ KUMĀRABHŪTĀYA BODHISATVĀYA MAHĀSATTVĀYA MAHĀKĀRUNIKĀYA / TAD YATHĀ / OṂ NIRĀLAMBE NIRĀBHASE JAYA JAYA LABHE MAHĀMATE DAKṢHE DAKṢHIṆI ME PARIŚHODHĀYA SVĀHĀ
>
> *By saying this dharaṇi even once, one completely purifies alms as vast as Mount Meru. This dharaṇi is taken from the "Dulwa Nampar Ngepe Gyu".*

That section is something that is traditionally said after a meal for the benefit of the donors of a meal. It is in Sanskrit and has two parts. The first part, ***I prostrate to the bhagavat, tathāgata, arhat, samyaksaṃbuddha Samantaprabhārāja*** is a homage. The second part *NAMAḤ ... PARIŚODHĀYA SVĀHĀ* is called a dhāraṇī. Dhāraṇīs are quite similar to mantras but are usually much longer. The first part of the dhāraṇī "I prostrate to the bhagavat..." was kept both in translated and untranslated forms in the Tibetan liturgy. The English translation follows that. This means that when you recite the liturgy you are actually saying this first part twice, once in English and once, just following that, in Sanskrit. This first part is a homage to Lord Buddha, quite similar to the one at the very beginning of the liturgy, although in this case it is to one of his manifestations called Samantaprabhārāja. Samantaprabhārāja means "The Total Light King". The next part, *NAMO MAÑJUŚRĪ ... MAHĀKĀRUṆIKĀYA*, pays homage to Mañjuśhrī and then mentions his great qualities by listing some of his epithets. It means "Homage to Mañjuśhrī the youthful prince, the bodhisatva, the great being bodhisatva, the embodiment of great compassion". A "great being bodhisatva" is a bodhisatva who is on one of the pure bhumis—the eighth bhumi or higher. Bodhisatvas who have reached this level are regarded as extra special, because their realization surpasses that even of an arhat.

This practice evolved from the situation where a practitioner actually received his livelihood as a gift from others. Out of kindness, donors who had faith in practitioners would give up a portion of the fruits of their labours so that practitioners could have the freedom to concentrate on practice. From the practitioner's point of view, the proper intention in accepting the alms was to accept them solely for the sake of practice, and without any sense of using the hard work of others just to escape the need for working. The recipients of alms thus had two things to take care of: firstly, they were indebted to their patrons; and secondly, they had to deal with any negativity created in the acceptance or use of the alms. Saying the dhāraṇī takes care of both things. On the one hand, saying the dhāraṇī is done as a purification for the donors, so that their merit will increase and they will attain enlightenment. On the other hand, saying the dhāraṇī has the effect of purifying any negativity created by accepting or using the alms for less than an altruistic purpose. An illustration of this practice is contained in something Milarepa once said, after receiving and using alms food: "The patrons in the villages work hard, and, out of their faith, provide me with sustenance to practice the path. May their obscurations be purified, and my practice flourish, so that we might attain enlightenment together."

In the Shambhala community, few are real recipients of alms, but a little thought will show how the above idea applies. Whilst chanting this section, one should be mindful of the donors' kindnesses and think of helping them along the path by purifying their negativities and obstacles. And one should purify any of one's own negativity created by using the food for the wrong purpose. The text at the end of the dhāraṇī says, ***by saying this dhāraṇī even once, one completely purifies alms as vast as Mount Meru.*** Mt. Meru is a mountain of cosmic dimensions, often used as an example of the sheer size of something. The liturgy says that ***this dhāraṇī is taken from the Dulwa Nampar Ngepe Gyu***. The name of the text is given there in Tibetan. It is a Vinaya text.

5. Concluding Verses of Aspiration, Dedication, and Generosity

It is quite traditional to end any activity of awakening with aspirations for the increase of good qualities and to dedicate whatever wholesome energy has been aroused to the benefit of oneself and others. In fact, this is not just a matter of tradition but is done because of the way in which karma works. There are several very good reasons why one needs to dedicate merit as soon as it has been created.

The merit is dedicated here with two selections. The liturgy says:

Then, as is said in the Āgamas:

> *May the royal patron and likewise*
> *The other sentient beings who are donors*
> *Obtain long life, freedom from sickness, prosperity,*
> *And the companionship of eternal bliss.*

That and:

> *By this generosity one has power over the bhūtas.*
> *By this generosity one is free from enemies.*
> *Generosity is the transcendent friend.*
> *Therefore, generosity is said to be essential.*
>
> *Generosity is the ornament of the world.*

Through generosity, one turns back from the lower realms.
Generosity is the stairway to the higher realms.
Generosity is the virtue that produces peace.

The prosperity of the bodhisatvas
Is inexhaustible, filling the whole of space.
In order to obtain such prosperity,
Completely propagate that generosity.

Say these verses of dedication, aspiration, and generosity.

The first is a verse from the Āgamas, which is one of the twelve sections of the sutra basket. The Āgamas contain discourses given by the Buddha. This is a prayer of dedication for the people who provided the food, it being traditional that whenever someone provides alms, the merit involved is dedicated back to them. It was quite common for the kings who were patrons of the Buddha to provide a whole meal for the Buddha and all of his followers. This was usually arranged in advance in much the same way as setting up a luncheon date. Often, the meal would be provided in one of the large gardens donated by the kings who were patrons of the Buddha. At the conclusion of the meal, the Buddha and his retinue would dedicate the merit back to their royal patron and any other sentient beings who were donors of the food. The Buddha would rest for a while and then give a discourse or answer questions from the king or the other donors. In some ways it must have been similar to an Oryoki meal at seminary.

When you really understand the practice involved in a meal taken using this liturgy—whether you follow the outer form of Oryoki or not—you find that the whole session is a period of practising generosity. That is in fact how the liturgy is intended. If you study it carefully, you will see that it is not meant as a nice container for you to get on with the essential business of feeding your body. Rather, it is a way to turn your being into generosity for the whole session, beginning to end, and that the apparently pragmatic business of feeding yourself is also a practice of offering. This "feel" for the practice does not come immediately but it can be developed. You can start with the idea of being generous through the session and that can lead to the direct experience of the whole session being generosity in action, without interruption.

People have a tendency to think of parts of Oryoki as practising generosity but when you really understand Oryoki, the whole period, even the eating of food for yourself, is a practice of giving. If you come to that understanding and then have the actual experience of it, these ending verses take on a whole new light. They are not merely dedicatory verses or nice reminders but they serve to increase the feeling that has come with the practice of generosity so far.

You might find yourself bowing mentally as you recite the first verse—or actually bowing in fact in a private session of practice—to the cooks and anyone else involved in provision and preparation of the food you have eaten. A very powerful sense of the whole interdependency involved can arise and then appreciation for that. I have often found myself saying the words, "May the cooks and food providers and preparers truly have long life, freedom from sickness, prosperity, and the companionship of eternal bliss". At that point, it is not mere words or thought but heartfelt dedication of all the goodness that has been aroused by doing a session of the practice back to these worthy helpers. That in itself is yet more generosity, and it leads on to the remaining three verses.

The remaining three verses extol the virtues of generosity. As mentioned above, if you have really participated in the practice as a continuous practice of generosity, these verses take on much meaning as you recite them.

There are truly nasty, hungry ghost type spirits and there are also ones that have less power but just make trouble for their own reasons. These are the "bhūtas" mentioned in the verse and who have been discussed earlier. The trouble they cause often comes simply because you are their turf and it is bothering them so they do whatever they can to rectify it. The traditional solution for this has always been to make a food offering to the local owners, as they are called, of any place you inhabit, as well as expressing your good intentions and lack of interest in harming them. The protector prayers done each day by practitioners are supposed to include this kind of offering and statement to the bhūtas who are the local owners. When you make offerings to them, many of them stop being a hindrance, if that is what they were doing, and either go their own way, or even become helpers. You have, as part of the session, made offerings to a wide range of bhūtas so you are reminding yourself here that such generosity gives you the ability to control any menace that they might present, let alone use them as helpers. Again, if you really have connected with the session of eating as wall-to-wall generosity, this line will make a lot of sense, and you can find yourself rejoicing as you say this in the usefulness of generosity.

Being a generous person, you will tend to have fewer enemies, not the least for the simple fact that generous people are usually well liked. Generosity itself is the very best of friends, is the meaning of the next line. Altogether, for this life, generosity is the most important thing to have, is what the verse is saying.

The next verse points out how valuable generosity is from a perspective of other lives and even enlightenment which transcends samsaric life. It prevents birth in the lower realms, is the means by which one takes birth in any of the higher realms, and, not only that, but is one of the key virtues that leads to the peace of the arhats and buddhas. Note the progression: the first two lines remind you that generosity keeps you out of the bad places of cyclic existence and lets you ascend to its good places, whereas the third line reminds you that generosity is one of the key virtues that leads you out of cyclic existence to the peace of enlightenment.

The last verse moves specifically to a Great Vehicle approach. There is here a little problem with the translation. What the verse actually says is, "What bodhisatvas have for their use is, like space, unending, so, if you want that for yourself, you should genuinely get on with the development of generosity".

Again, if you have the experience of the whole session having been generosity in action, these verses will have great impact as you say them. The truth of them will come home strongly.

There are other versions of the meal liturgy with a longer set of dedication prayers for the donors than given here. These longer prayers are part of the standard prayers used by monks and nuns to make dedications for the donors.

That is the end of the Tibetan monastic meal liturgy and the end of the liturgy as used in Oryoki. The liturgy as presented by Dudjom Rinpoche has a small addendum for making a meal into an inner feast practice as described in the chapter introducing the liturgy.

Index